◁□▷

Confrontations
Derrida/Heidegger/Nietzsche

◁□▷

CONFRONTATIONS
Derrida/Heidegger/Nietzsche

ERNST BEHLER

Translated, with an Afterword, by
Steven Taubeneck

Stanford University Press
Stanford, California

Stanford University Press
Stanford, California
© 1991 by the Board of Trustees of the
Leland Stanford Junior University
Printed and bound by CPI Group
(UK) Ltd, Croydon, CR0 4YY

Confrontations: Derrida/Heidegger/Nietzsche
was originally published in German in 1988
under the title *Derrida-Nietzsche, Nietzsche-
Derrida*, © 1988 by Verlag Ferdinand
Schöningh, Paderborn. The Translator's
Afterword was prepared specially for this
edition by Steven Taubeneck.

CIP data are at the end of the book

◁□▷

Contents

◁□▷

Preface to the English Edition

Our image of the "new Nietzsche" as it has emerged since the late 1960's finds perhaps its most suggestive expression in the writings of Jacques Derrida. Nietzsche, as explored by Derrida, offers a new kind of communication, one that resists the temptation to posit fixed doctrines or ultimate meanings but persists in the endless deciphering of its own terms. Derrida highlights Nietzsche's turn toward infinite interpretation, or the affirmation of a view of the world as play, and shows how the style in which such thinking manifests itself must be plural. Yet in his insistence on these attitudes, Derrida necessarily challenges Martin Heidegger's interpretation of Nietzsche as the thinker of the most condensed notion of modern metaphysics, the "will to power." For Heidegger, Nietzsche's "will to power" epitomizes the metaphysics of the subject and represents the ultimate inversion of Plato's "ideas." Derrida views Heidegger's reading of Nietzsche as an extreme type of truth-oriented, unifying, and systematizing hermeneutics that, because of its own attachments to metaphysics, misconstrues the multiple subtleties of Nietzsche's text in a highly reductionist manner. Indeed, Derrida disputes Heidegger in each of his writings, and the confrontation is always, directly or indirectly, bound up with Nietzsche.

The most provocative aspect of these confrontations lies not just in the spectacle of a contest in Nietzsche interpretation and

Nietzsche philology, but in the ongoing attempt to press the limits of philosophy and writing. Drawn into this debate as if he were their contemporary, Nietzsche dominates the sequence of names entitling this book, for he heralds a kind of critical thinking that has become more urgently our own: the critique of thought, an auto-critique of philosophy.

When this book first appeared in German, I meant to convey aspects of Derrida's writing to the German reading public via Nietzsche's texts. This required a considerable discussion of Heidegger's interpretation of Nietzsche. Whereas the German title emphasized my original intention, the English title was chosen to underline the process of critique at work here, and marked by the names of Derrida, Heidegger, and Nietzsche. I am grateful to my colleague Steven Taubeneck for having so carefully rendered the German text in English.

Ernst Behler   April 1991
Seattle

◁☐▷

Note on the Citations

As much as possible, citations of English-language works and translations have been substituted for the citations of German- and French-language works in the German edition. The following abbreviations are used in the text and notes:

BAT   Martin Heidegger, *Being and Time*, trans. John Macquarrie and Edward Robinson (New York: Harper & Row, 1962).

BGE   Friedrich Nietzsche, *Beyond Good and Evil*, trans. Walter Kaufmann (New York: Random House, 1966).

BP   Martin Heidegger, *The Basic Problems of Phenomenology*, trans. Albert Hofstadter (Bloomington: Indiana University Press, 1982).

BT   Friedrich Nietzsche, *The Birth of Tragedy and the Case of Wagner*, trans. Walter Kaufmann (New York: Random House, 1967).

BW   Martin Heidegger, *Basic Writings*, ed. David Farrell Krell (New York: Harper & Row, 1977).

C   Allan Bloom, *The Closing of the American Mind* (New York: Simon & Schuster, 1987).

CIS   Richard Rorty, *Contingency, Irony, and Solidarity* (Cambridge, Eng.: Cambridge University Press, 1989).

D   Friedrich Nietzsche, *Daybreak*, trans. R. J. Hollingdale (Cambridge, Eng.: Cambridge University Press, 1982).

DD   Diane P. Michelfelder and Richard E. Palmer, eds., *Dialogue and Deconstruction: The Gadamer-Derrida Encounter* (Albany: State University of New York Press, 1989).

DM   Jürgen Habermas, *The Philosophical Discourse of Moder-*
        nity, trans. Frederick Lawrence (Cambridge, Mass.: MIT
        Press, 1987).

DS   Jacques Derrida, *Dissemination*, trans. Barbara Johnson
        (Chicago: University of Chicago Press, 1981).

DTM   Walter Kaufmann, *Discovering the Mind*, vol. 2, *Nietzsche,*
        Heidegger, and Buber (New York: McGraw-Hill, 1980).

EP   Martin Heidegger, *The End of Philosophy*, trans. Joan
        Stambaugh (New York: Harper & Row, 1973).

G   Jacques Derrida, *Of Grammatology*, trans. Gayatri Chakra-
        vorty Spivak (Baltimore: Johns Hopkins University Press,
        1976).

GM   Friedrich Nietzsche, *On the Genealogy of Morals and Ecce*
        Homo, trans. Walter Kaufmann and R. J. Hollingdale (New
        York: Random House, 1969).

GS   Friedrich Nietzsche, *The Gay Science*, trans. Walter Kauf-
        mann (New York: Random House, 1974).

HW   Jacques Derrida, *Husserls Weg in die Geschichte am Leit-*
        faden der Geometrie: Ein Kommentar zur Beilage III der
        "Krise," trans. Rüdiger Hentschel and Andreas Knop (Mu-
        nich: Fink, 1987).

KGB   Friedrich Nietzsche, *Kritische Gesamtausgabe der Briefe*, ed.
        Giorgio Colli and Mazzino Montinari. 16 vols. (Berlin:
        de Gruyter, 1984).

KSA   Friedrich Nietzsche, *Kritische Studienausgabe*, ed. Giorgio
        Colli and Mazzino Montinari. 15 vols. (Berlin: de Gruyter,
        1984).

LI   Maurice Blanchot, *L'Entretien infini* (Paris: Garnier,
        1969).

MP   Jacques Derrida, *Margins of Philosophy*, trans. Alan Bass
        (Chicago: University of Chicago Press, 1982).

N   Martin Heidegger, *Nietzsche*, trans. David Farrell Krell,
        Joan Stambaugh, Frank A. Capuzzi. 4 vols. (San Francisco:
        Harper & Row, 1979–87).

NANS   "Nietzsche and Allan Bloom's Nietzsche: A Symposium,"
        in *Nietzscheana #1*, ed. Richard Schacht (Urbana, Ill.:
        1989).

NFM   Michel Foucault, "Nietzsche, Freud, Marx," *Cahiers de*
        Royaumont: Philosophie, no. 6 (1967): 183–92.

NGH Michel Foucault, "Nietzsche, Genealogy, History," in *The Foucault Reader*, ed. Paul Rabinow (New York: Pantheon Books, 1984), 76–100.

NO Jacques Derrida, "Nietzsches Otobiographie oder Politik des Eigennamens," *Fugen: Deutsch-Französisches Jahrbuch für Text-Analytik* 1980, 64–98.

NPPA Walter Kaufmann, *Nietzsche: Philosopher, Psychologist, Antichrist*, 4th ed. (Princeton: Princeton University Press, 1974).

OG Edmund Husserl, *L'origine de la géométrie*, trans., with an introduction, Jacques Derrida (Paris: Presses Universitaires de France, 1962).

OS Jacques Derrida, *Of Spirit: Heidegger and the Question*, trans. Geoffrey Bennington and Rachel Bowlby (Chicago: University of Chicago Press, 1989).

OTB Martin Heidegger, *On Time and Being*, trans. Joan Stambaugh (New York: Harper & Row, 1972).

P Jacques Derrida, *Positions*, trans. Alan Bass (Chicago: University of Chicago Press, 1981).

QB Martin Heidegger, *The Question of Being* [*Zur Seinsfrage*], trans. William Klubach and Jean T. Wilde (New York: Twayne, 1958).

QT Martin Heidegger, *The Question Concerning Technology and Other Essays*, trans. William Lovitt (New York: Harper & Row, 1977).

SNS Jacques Derrida, *Spurs: Nietzsche's Styles*, trans. Barbara Harlow (Chicago: University of Chicago Press, 1978).

SP Jacques Derrida, *"Speech and Phenomena" and Other Essays on Husserl's Theory of Signs*, trans. David B. Allison (Evanston, Ill.: Northwestern University Press, 1973).

TI Friedrich Nietzsche, *Twilight of the Idols*, trans. R. J. Hollingdale (Baltimore: Penguin, 1968).

TT Jacques Derrida, "The Time of a Thesis: Punctuations," in *Philosophy in France Today*, ed. Alan Montefiore (Cambridge, Eng.: Cambridge University Press, 1983), 34–50.

TUI Philippe Forget, ed., *Text und Interpretation: Deutsch-französische Debatte mit Beiträgen von J. Derrida, Ph. Forget, H. Frank, H.-G. Gadamer, J. Greisch und F. Laruelle* (Munich: Fink, 1984).

WD   Jacques Derrida, *Writing and Difference*, trans. Alan Bass
      (Chicago: University of Chicago Press, 1978).
WM   Hans-Georg Gadamer, *Wahrheit und Methode*, 4th ed. (Tü-
      bingen: Mohr, 1975).

◁□▷

Confrontations
Derrida/Heidegger/Nietzsche

◁☐▷

Introduction

Undoubtedly it would be useful to interpret the "new Nietzsche," as he is often called, within the larger contexts of "Nietzsche and the metaphysical tradition" or "Nietzsche in the
twentieth century."[1] An historical series of successively developing images could better dissolve the systematic linkage of
Nietzsche to the metaphysical interpretations of his texts than
any subtle, textual critique of such relations. Moreover, no examination of Derrida's readings of Nietzsche would be complete without an analysis of their new, modern or postmodern
components, an examination that also requires an investigation
of larger historical connections. Nietzsche himself directly ad-
vocates such a rigorously eschatological approach to his texts,
and here presumably lies one of the reasons his writing is perceived today as the "entry into postmodernity." *Beyond Good
and Evil*, with its subtitle *Prelude to a Philosophy of the Future*
and its repeated addresses to the "coming" philosophers or the
philosophers of the "coming" century, is a characteristic text
for this thinking in historical terms.

There are, in other words, good reasons for situating Der-

[1] Cf. David B. Allison, ed., *The New Nietzsche: Contemporary Styles of
Interpretation* (New York: Delta, 1977). See also Werner Hamacher, ed.,
*Nietzsche aus Frankreich: Essays von Maurice Blanchot, Jacques Derrida,
Pierre Klossowski, Philippe Lacoue-Labarthe, Jean-Luc Nancy und Bernard
Pautrat* (Frankfurt and Berlin: Ullstein, 1986).

rida's Nietzsche within the contemporary framework. Indeed, Nietzsche is often read in such a manner. His impact as a writer began around the turn of the twentieth century. During the first half of the century he was one of the most influential and widely read authors, and his name enjoyed a meteoric rise in popularity. During World War II, however, and especially after its end, interest in Nietzsche lessened. Thomas Mann, in a 1947 address to the Pen Club of Zürich entitled "Nietzsche's Philosophy in the Light of Our Experience," described the attitude of that time toward Nietzsche as one of "lamentation" and captured this mood in his novel *Doctor Faustus*.[2] Nietzsche's prominence in the contemporary world has been revived by a number of recent interpretations, particularly Derrida's reading.

One major reason these attempts at updating and the apocalyptic or historical aspects are not emphasized here is that too little is known about Nietzsche's reception during the twentieth century. This includes his reception in literature, which became more intensively engaged with Nietzsche than did academic philosophy. Especially important here are those authors "in Vienna, in St. Petersburg, in Stockholm, in Copenhagen, in Paris, in New York" who, Nietzsche said as early as 1888 in a puzzling comment, had "discovered" him (*GM*, 262). He referred specifically to poets but also to all writers "dominated by literature," "fanatics of *expression* 'at any price,'" as he described them (*BGE*, 197). To be sure, our ability to understand Nietzsche is inhibited by the fact that his texts transgress the boundaries typically dividing academic disciplines, but this blurring of genres has also had a stimulating effect. Derrida, for example, avoids the reductions possible in a strictly philosophical reading of Nietzsche by drawing attention to the heterogeneity of his writing. In any case, the preliminary studies

[2] Thomas Mann, "Nietzsches Philosophie im Lichte der heutigen Erfahrung," in idem, *Reden und Aufsätze: Gesammelte Werke in 12 Bänden* (Frankfurt: S. Fischer, 1960), 9: 675–713.

for a comparative analysis in terms of the poetry and literature of the twentieth century still need to be done.

The primary reason why Derrida's readings of Nietzsche do not appear here against the background of "today" or "postmodernity" is that his approach does not follow from such a perspective. Reading Nietzsche in terms of the history of metaphysics and ontology was Heidegger's approach. An image of Nietzsche as "the last metaphysician" or "the last philosopher" follows predictably from such a reading. Derrida approaches Nietzsche with a structuralist, grammatological, and biographical analysis of his text. He reads Nietzsche not in order to classify him or to situate him somewhere, but to explore his text. Concepts such as "the last metaphysician" or "the last philosopher" seem absurd from such a perspective, as would other rigidly categorical assumptions when applied to this writing. From his structuralist, grammatological, biographical, and resolutely non-ontological perspective, Derrida avoids fixation on a selection, compilation, or manipulation of Nietzsche's writings, such as that which resulted in *The Will to Power*, and considers instead the texts often overlooked in philosophical readings: those figurative, ironic examples of indirect communication published by Nietzsche himself. Of course, the emphasis on Nietzsche the writer instead of Nietzsche the ontological metaphysician will not result in a conclusive reading unless it also considers the metaphysical dimension. In contrast to the Nietzsche found in the voluminous interpretations written from the perspective of the history of ontology, Derrida's Nietzsche may seem unusually light and capricious. But this impression should not obscure which Nietzsche is at stake: the ironically skeptical writer rather than the dogmatic visionary of power.

In addition, however, it is not only Nietzsche that is at stake here—it is also Derrida and Heidegger. Written relatively early in his career and appearing in the 1970's and early 1980's, Derrida's writings on Nietzsche provide an excellent starting point for understanding his critique of philosophy, especially in relation to Heidegger. The most famous example from this complex, *Spurs: Nietzsche's Styles* (1972), is one of the first instances of that expository, mise-en-scène style of writing characteristic of Derrida's later texts. In his early writings, Derrida frequently employed the alienating, cool, value-free discourse of recent linguistics, following the conceptual model of formal semiological procedures. Already by 1967 in *Grammatology*, however, this discourse merges with one derived from Nietzsche, Freud, and Heidegger, and leads to the same epochal break: the activity of the sign without truth, without foundation, without beginning and end. We could also refer to these largely negative designations as the infinite, playful exchangeability of signs. It is this capacity that Nietzsche termed the *Dionysian*.

Nietzsche is of fundamental importance for Derrida, whose discourse is determined to an extraordinary degree by German writers, particularly Freud, Hegel, Kafka, Celan, Kant, and most of all Heidegger. Many see Derrida's work as essentially a continuation of Heidegger's philosophy; others see Derrida's early writing on Husserl as his best book (see, e.g., *SP*). Of all Derrida's confrontations with German intellectual history, however, Nietzsche's texts are perhaps the most decisive. This is shown most clearly in one of Derrida's first writings, his 1966 debate with Claude Lévi-Strauss. Toward the end of this essay, Derrida addresses two kinds of thinking. The first is structuralism, which could also be linked to philosophical hermeneutics, philosophical communications theory, and any form of revisionist Hegelianism. In this type of thinking, the concept of "origin" goes hand in hand with that of "goal." The second kind is represented by Derrida himself and is characteristically bound up with Nietzsche:

There are thus two interpretations of interpretations, of structure, of sign, of play. The one seeks to decipher, dreams of deciphering a truth or an origin which escapes play and the order of the sign, and which lives the necessity of interpretation as an exile. The other, which is no longer turned toward the origin, affirms play and tries to

pass beyond man and humanism, the name of man being the name
of that being who, throughout the history of metaphysics or of
onto-theology—in other words, throughout his entire history—has
dreamed of full presence, the reassuring foundation, the origin and
the end of play.³

For these reasons, Derrida's interpretations of Nietzsche do
not produce an historically developing account, or a commentary on Nietzsche in the manner of a progressively developing philosophical self-consciousness. Those two conceptions
would construct an image of continual development toward
congruence, coherence, and gradual integration, one that
somehow produces a totality. Derrida's reading of Nietzsche
operates, by contrast, in a disruptive manner, against the domi-
nant image of Nietzsche of the 1960's and 1970's, particularly
as it is developed with great emphasis, scope, and reiteration in
Heidegger's *Nietzsche*. If one still wants to find an entry point
into deconstruction from the perspective of the history of science and to situate it further in terms of the history of philosophy or simply of generations, then there are occasional references to consider in the writings of Derrida. But their casual
character gives the impression that he does not see these issues
as particularly important or, at least, not as an important topic
for deconstruction.

The historico-scientific dimension is perhaps most explicitly
addressed at the beginning of *Grammatology*. There Derrida
deals with all the consequences arising from a science of writing and the signs of writing, as if his intent were to conclude
the preceding historico-metaphysical epoch. In place of the historical and hierarchical system of ordering from the tradition
of Western metaphysics, the free play of signs among themselves would emerge. He presents Saussure and Heidegger as
pioneers of this effort (*G*, 10–65). Saussure promoted it with
his structuralist view of language, which distinguishes the

³Jacques Derrida, "Structure, Sign, and Play in the Discourse of the Human Sciences," in *WD*, 278–93.

value of linguistic signs only by means of the differences among them, the negative differences from each other in the network of language. Heidegger distinguished in metaphysical thought the multiplicity of beings from their ground and thus raised the possibility of examining the free, playful interchangeability of beings among themselves. But both missed the way out of metaphysics: Saussure, since he privileged the human voice or the phonic substance, and Heidegger, since he sought the presence of Being through modes of forgetting Being and mourning its absence. Nevertheless, in both thinkers there appeared something of the explosive power, something of the "trembling" and uncertainty distinctive of "all post-Hegelian attempts and to this passage between two epochs" (*G*, 24).

In "Structure, Sign, and Play," Derrida represents this epochal break as a "rupture" in thought and asks when this "decentering" occurred and who brought it about. But to refer "to an event, a doctrine, or an author" would be "somewhat naive," he writes, since such an event belongs to "the totality of an era" and, more precisely, "has always already begun to proclaim itself and begun to *work*" (*WD*, 280). If one nevertheless chose several "names," "as indications only," in order to find the authors "in whose discourse this occurrence has kept most closely to its most radical formulation," then certainly the names of Nietzsche, Freud, and Heidegger would have to be mentioned: Nietzsche for his "critique of metaphysics, the critique of the concepts of Being and truth," for which he "substituted the concepts of play, interpretation, and sign (sign without present truth)"; Freud, because of his "critique of self-presence, that is, the critique of consciousness, of the subject, of self-identity and of self-proximity or self-possession"; and Heidegger, because of his "destruction of metaphysics, of onto-theology, of the determination of Being as presence" (*WD*, 280).

Already in *Grammatology*, Derrida argues that all these "destructive discourses" are "trapped in a kind of circle"

(*WD*, 280). He maintains that one cannot approach the pre-established structures of metaphysics "from the outside" (*G*, 24). One can have a decisive impact only by inhabiting these structures: "Operating necessarily from the inside, borrowing all the strategic and economic resources of subversion from the old structure, borrowing them structurally, that is to say without being able to isolate their elements and atoms, the enterprise of deconstruction always in a certain way falls prey to its own work" (*G*, 24). In his essay on structure and play, Derrida concludes: "There is no sense in doing without the concepts of metaphysics in order to shake metaphysics. We have no language—no syntax and no lexicon—which is foreign to this history; we can pronounce not a single destructive proposition which has not already had to slip into the form, the logic, and the implicit postulations of precisely what it seeks to contest" (*WD*, 280–81). This has unavoidable consequences for deconstructive discourse, insofar as each linguistic or conceptual borrowing always calls forth "the entire metaphysics" and, in the process, falls prey to deconstruction itself. Without excluding himself, Derrida states: "This is what allows these destroyers to destroy each other reciprocally—for example, Heidegger regarding Nietzsche, with as much lucidity and rigor as bad faith and misconstruction, as the last metaphysician, the last 'Platonist.' One could do the same for Heidegger himself, for Freud, or for a number of others. And today no exercise is more widespread" (*WD*, 281–82).

Attempts to overcome metaphysics occur in discourses directly critical of metaphysics as well as in a wide range of indirectly critical analyses, exercises in circumvention and avoidance in which the distinctive practices of the epoch reveal themselves. Bricolage—the pragmatic application of concepts and methods without an inherent truth claim, as "mere instrument"—is such an attempt (*WD*, 285), and the reconstruction of conceptual histories tries to move beyond philosophy (*WD*, 280). Yet to go beyond philosophy does not always mean to close the book of philosophy, an act that leads in most cases to poor philosophizing, but to continue "to read philosophers *in a certain way*" (*WD*, 288). The "nominalism" and the caution in the contemporary philosophical manner of expression also manifest an enormous amount of deconstruction, though not usually under this name. The same could be said of the self-critical awareness of mythopoetic elements in philosophical discourse.

With these exemplary turns commenced the epochal break, or the attempt at a transgression of the epoch, beginning at the outset of the twentieth century and accelerating through the following decades and generations. In the 1968 essay "The Ends of Man" Derrida characterized the situation more specifically, as he described the philosophical scene in France shortly after World War II and analogous developments in other countries (*MP*, 109–36). As a characteristic feature of these early postwar years, a new beginning in intellectual terms, Derrida stressed the commonly held view that the "unity of human reality" formed the stabilizing ground of philosophical argumentation. This was, in any case, the shared feature of atheistic and Christian Existentialism, humanisms from left and right, Marxism, Social Democracy, and Christian Democracy as well as the anthropological readings of Hegel, Husserl, and Heidegger. The alleged reality of the human subject or of human individuality was the unquestioned presupposition of this time; everything occurred "as if the sign 'man' had no origin, no historical, cultural, or linguistic limit" (*MP*, 116). Heidegger's *Letter on Humanism* had emphasized specifically that every humanism remains metaphysical. But Heidegger and even Nietzsche were, at that time, interpreted humanistically.

For these reasons, Derrida resists characterizing epochs and his occasional remarks in this area are more of an anecdotal kind. He in no way claims to exhaust an epoch with his observations, nor to say that a certain period began after the war "and even less that it is over today" (*MP*, 117). But one trait that does perhaps distinguish our time from previous times is that it is no longer acceptable to speak of the fixed, enduring reality of human beings, the human subject or the individual, in a self-assured manner. Derrida describes this change more precisely in a short autobiographical text that outlines the preceding thirty years of academic philosophy in France, which have many parallels in other countries. Here the turning point is located in the dramatic year of 1968, a year in which the predominance of structuralism in anthropological, historical, linguistic, literary, and psychoanalytic disciplines began to dissolve, a year when the static authority of the Gaullist republic began to unravel and the institutional traditions of the Sorbonne began to disintegrate (*TT*, 41).

When the question of overcoming metaphysics is raised directly, however, Derrida's answers are negative or, in any case, not affirmative. One possible answer consists in the distinction between "closure" (*clôture*) and "end" (*fin*) (*G*, 4, 14). What is conceptualized as a comprehensive closure, such as the end of metaphysics, the end of philosophy, or the end of man, can persist infinitely, just as it has "always already" (*toujours déjà*) begun and announced its effects. Another answer consists in his concept of "transgression," which is to be understood both in the spatiotemporal sense and as the violation of a prohibition. The transgression occurring at the closure does not land somewhere beyond metaphysics; rather, it persists endlessly in the unavoidable grasp of metaphysics. On this point Derrida comments:

There is *not* a transgression, if one understands by that a pure and simple landing into a beyond of metaphysics, at a point which also would be, let us not forget, first of all a point of language or writing. Now, even in aggressions or transgressions, we are consorting with a code to which metaphysics is tied irreducibly, such that every transgressive gesture reencloses us—precisely by giving us a hold on the closure of metaphysics—within this closure. But by means of the work done on one side and the other of the limit the field inside is modified, and a transgression is produced that consequently is no-where present as a *fait accompli*. One is never installed within trans-gression, one never lives elsewhere. Transgression implies that the limit is always at work.   (*P*, 12)

Nietzsche was profoundly important for these develop-ments in postwar philosophy. Heidegger's *Nietzsche* appeared in 1961 and immediately sparked a lively debate in Germany as well as in France regarding not only the interpretation of Nietzsche but also philosophizing in general. In Germany es-pecially, the systematic and systematizing Nietzsche interpre-tations of the 1960's and 1970's were linked directly to Heideg-ger. These began with the central question that perhaps every interpretation of Nietzsche must raise; namely, whether the philosopher's aphoristic and fragmentary text, which appar-ently rejects final principles and systematic coherence, never-theless can be read in the style of traditional metaphysics. One example from the many attempts to frame this question and its possible answers can be found in the work of Walter Schulz, who argued "that Nietzsche undertook, despite or perhaps precisely because of his strict opposition to classical metaphys-ics, to understand for himself the totality of beings as a unity, that is, to interpret it on the basis of one principle around which the interpreter must organize all his concerns, and on this basis he can organize himself, or, in other words, his own thought and action."[4]

If we consider Nietzsche's many statements about the "gen-eral starting point of his thoughts," Schulz continues, then it seems that Nietzsche did radically devalue the "traditional metaphysics of reason," but only in favor of a new metaphysics, a "metaphysics of life," a "metaphysical sanctioning of in-stincts." Metaphysics, for Schulz, is always directed toward an absolute. Traditionally this absolute was God. The space left

[4]Walter Schulz, "Funktion und Ort der Kunst in Nietzsches Philoso-phie," *Nietzsche-Studien* 12 (1983): 2–3.

vacant by the death of God was occupied by man. Since Nietzsche identified man as the determining figure, he remained within the "scheme of traditional metaphysics." Of course, according to Schulz, Nietzsche saw that the time in which man believed in independent values was past. From this insight, however, Nietzsche did not achieve a real overcoming of metaphysics, which might correspond to the situation of contemporary human beings alienated from metaphysics, but realized only the "absolute demand for new values."[5] For Schulz, the end of this tradition is first achieved by Heidegger. In fact Heidegger's philosophy proved to be, if one understands it historically or in the context of Western metaphysics, the "innermost conclusion of the event of Western metaphysics." Metaphysics appears in this perspective as "the completion of an event already meaningful in itself" with a "determinate development that pushes toward an end," an end that "is reached in our time and becomes visible in Heidegger's philosophy."[6]

In the French reception of Nietzsche during these years, probably under the influence of Heidegger, the themes of overturning, "twisting out," or in a melancholy sense "overcoming the loss" of metaphysics become quite prominent. Heidegger treats these themes most specifically in the section "Nietzsche's Overturning of Platonism" from the first lecture series of 1936–37, "The Will to Power as Art" (*N*, 1: 200–210). Heidegger draws in this context on the aphorism from the *Twilight of the Idols* entitled "How the 'Real World' at Last Became a Myth: History of an Error," which depicts the abolition of the true world and of truth ("I, Plato, *am* the truth") in the six levels of history of European philosophy (*"with the real world*

[5]Walter Schulz, "Nietzsche: Die metaphysische Sanktionierung der Triebschicht," in idem, *Philosophie in der veränderten Welt* (Pfullingen: Neske, 1976), 408–18.

[6]Walter Schulz, "Über den philosophiegeschichtlichen Ort Martin Heideggers," in *Heidegger: Perspektiven zur Deutung seines Werks*, ed. Otto Pöggeler (Cologne and Berlin: Kiepenheuer und Witsch, 1970), 95–139.

we have also abolished the apparent world!") (*TI*, 40–41). The fable closely resembles Heidegger's own narrative of the Western history of Being. Furthermore, the passage has found widespread resonance in recent French interpretations of Nietzsche. Heidegger reads the aphorism entirely in the sense of this history and sees all the phases of Nietzsche's "history of Platonism" arranged in such a way "that the 'true world,' the existence and legitimacy of which is under consideration, is in each division brought into connection with the type of man who comports himself in that world" (*N*, 1: 208).

The last step in this process, however, no longer coincides with Heidegger's usual interpretation of the text as the mere "overturning" of Platonism, but must be seen as the "twisting free" or disengagement from the whole complex. The abolition of the "true world" ("the supersensuous") together with the "apparent world" ("the sensuous") involves "the totality of beings" and thus is not merely a new level in the history of Being, but a complete revaluation of all previous values. As Heidegger says:

A path must be cleared for a new interpretation of the sensuous on the basis of a new hierarchy of the sensuous and nonsensuous. The new hierarchy does not simply wish to reverse matters within the old structural order, now reverencing the sensuous and scorning the nonsensuous. It does not wish to put what was at the very bottom on the very top. A new hierarchy and new valuation mean that the ordering structure must be changed. To that extent, overturning Platonism must become a twisting free of it.   (*N*, 1: 209–10)

Heidegger questions Nietzsche's role in this process and defers a decision to the time "when we have reflected in accordance with the thought that Nietzsche most intrinsically willed— beyond everything captious, ambiguous, and deficient which we might very easily ascribe to him here" (*N*, 1: 210). This amounts to saying that, with the doctrine of the will to power, Nietzsche has not achieved such a step. By contrast, French criticism of Nietzsche has consistently turned to those very elements in Nietzsche described by Heidegger as "everything captious, ambiguous, and deficient." Indeed, the same passage from *Twilight of the Idols* has received a generally positive reading in recent French criticism. Of course, we can sketch only the general directions of research at any given time in terms of such specific themes. But to give an impression of another reading of Nietzsche in contrast to the systematizing perspective, particularly in regard to his "masterpiece of philosophical prose" (Elisabeth Förster-Nietzsche), it is useful to mention the work of Maurice Blanchot. The debate over the reliability of the edition of those writings issued as *The Will to Power* was raised again in the 1950's by Richard Roos and Karl Schlechta and led to the new critical edition of the manuscripts by Mazzino Montinari.[7] In the course of these discussions, it became clear how the posthumous writings in the Nietzsche Archives had been organized and how the text of *The Will to Power* had been fabricated. This text was hailed from the outset as Nietzsche's philosophical masterpiece, and it was suggested that he had hidden his true philosophy in his published writings, that his real arguments were to be found in the unpublished fragments (*N*, 1: 9–10). Although Nietzsche's published writings often rely on aphoristic statements, this self-critical or self-ironizing manner of writing is lacking in his notebooks. Given

[7]Richard Roos, "Les derniers écrits de Nietzsche et leur publication," *Revue de philosophie* 146 (1956): 262–87; Karl Schlechta, "Philologischer Nachbericht," in Friedrich Nietzsche, *Werke in drei Bänden*, ed. K. Schlechta (Munich: Hanser, 1954–56), 3: 1383–432. The problematic quality of these editions had already been indicated in the 1930's: see H. J. Mette, *Der handschriftliche Nachlass Friedrich Nietzsches* (Leipzig, 1932); and idem, "Sachlicher Vorbericht zur Gesamtausgabe der Werke Friedrich Nietzsches," in Friedrich Nietzsche, *Werke und Briefe: Historisch-kritische Gesamtausgabe* (Munich: Beck, 1933), 1: cxxi-cxxii. On this topic, also see Mazzino Montinari, "Nietzsches Nachlass von 1885 bis 1888, oder Textkritik und *Wille zur Macht*," in idem, *Nietzsche lesen* (Berlin: de Gruyter, 1982), 92–119; and idem, *KSA*, 14: 383–400.

this situation, Blanchot began to inquire into the nature of Nietzsche's writing, emphasizing his particular topic of "écriture fragmentaire."[8] The specific question that sparks Blanchot's reflections, however, is why it had seemed necessary, or what the motivation had been, to produce a text that was after all nothing but a fabrication, falsification, or fraud. His answer is that it was assumed that a "great philosopher" would naturally leave behind a "masterpiece" presenting his "philosophy" systematically. The writings published by Nietzsche himself were obviously much too self-contradictory and aphoristic, much too frivolous and literary. Heidegger was perfectly aware of the fabricated character of *The Will to Power* and yet used it to encourage the systematizing interpretation of Nietzsche. Blanchot, who was well acquainted with Heidegger's *Nietzsche*, refers to Heidegger's dismissive statements about "the so-called major work" (*N*, 3: 10–14) that contains a "mixing" of passages "from many different periods" (*N*, 3: 13). From this, however, arose for Heidegger the obligation "to reflect on [Nietzsche's] thinking" (*N*, 1: 5) and to make the effort to think the central thought inscribed in the configuration of "the will to power." Of course, Blanchot argued, we can organize Nietzsche's contradictions coherently, especially if we arrange them in a hierarchical, dialectical, or Hegelian manner to facilitate a coherent reading. But even if we assume such a continuous discourse as the background for Nietzsche's discontinuous writings, we sense Nietzsche's dissatisfaction with that. His discourse is always already a step ahead of itself. He shelters his philosophy by exhibiting and formulating it in a completely different language, a language no longer assured of the whole, but consisting of fragments, conflicting points, and division. According to his own account, Blanchot wrote his notes on

---

[8]Maurice Blanchot, "Nietzsche et l'écriture fragmentaire," in *LI*, 227–55. For a German translation of the article, see *Nietzsche aus Frankreich* (cited in note 1 above), 47–73.

fragmentary writing in the margins of certain books about Nietzsche that appeared in 1969 by writers such as Michel Foucault, Gilles Deleuze, Eugen Fink, Jean Granier, and Jacques Derrida. What characterizes the "parole de fragment"? A few traits can be marked. Fragmentary writing is in the first place the rejection of system, a passion for the incomplete, the pursuit of unfinished movements of thought. It avoids self-complacency and accepts fragmentariness as the risk of a thinking that can no longer guarantee unity. Fragmentary writing also ignores contradiction; more positively stated, it expresses multiplicity, though not in a dialectical manner but in the borderless manner of difference. This difference is a distinct form of pluralism, neither multiple nor unitary, but governed by a certain kind of discontinuity. For Blanchot, such discontinuity marks a great turning point in the history of thought, a turn carried out by Nietzsche but ignored by all those commentators who try to "Hegelianize" him.

◁□▷

I

Heidegger

The many oscillations in Heidegger's reading of Nietzsche appear in the interpretation of the aphorism "How the 'Real World' at Last Became a Myth: History of an Error" (*N*, 1: 200–210). Nevertheless Heidegger's *Nietzsche*, a compilation of his lectures and manuscripts from 1936 to 1946 published in 1961, presents the most comprehensive, self-enclosed interpretation of Nietzsche yet produced. Heidegger limits his interpretation to a single philosophical principle, the will to power, and derives his general themes from that principle. This principle does not appear simply in the concept of "the will to power"; it emerges only if we think of the apparently irreconcilable thoughts of "the will to power" and "the eternal recurrence of the same" together, and in such an intensive way that "in terms of metaphysics, in its modern phase and in the history of its end, both thoughts think the selfsame" (*N*, 3: 163). Fused together, these two thoughts become a "*sole* thought" (*N*, 3: 10), and with this thinking Nietzsche fulfills "the essence of modernity; now, for the first time, modernity comes into its own." Ultimately, "in the essential unity of the two thoughts, the metaphysics that is approaching consummation utters its final word" (*N*, 3: 163).

This "coming into its own," however, should not be thought of as a stage in a continuing Hegelian dialectic. Rather, it should be seen within Heidegger's distinctive oscillations; in Heideggerian terms, Nietzsche's philosophy is the completion of Western metaphysics. This thinking expresses not only the end of philosophy, its *eschaton*, but also its apocalypse as the unveiling of its meaning or, better, as the revelation of its meaninglessness. The concept of subjectivity in Western metaphysics, which reaches its highest expression in the will to power, is revealed as madness in the cycle of the eternal recurrence. For Heidegger, Nietzsche's metaphysics is therefore "not an overcoming of nihilism," but "the ultimate entanglement in nihilism." Through this entanglement "nihilism first becomes thoroughly complete in what it is." "Such utterly completed, perfect nihilism is the fulfillment of nihilism proper" (*N*, 4: 203).

Prior to these lectures Nietzsche had not received much attention in the discipline of philosophy: he was mentioned with distant respect as a genial yet dangerous outsider. Even Heidegger, in his early *Being and Time*, treated Nietzsche only cursorily. Nietzsche's extraordinary dominance in European intellectual life during the prewar years was primarily literary and owed much to his poetic imagination. Stefan George and his followers elevated Nietzsche to the rank of a prophet, to the mythical anticipation of a new human being. André Gide saw Nietzsche as a deeply ambivalent figure caught between the overflowing, immoral celebration of life and the decadent, disillusioned nausea of existence. Thomas Mann interpreted Nietzsche in relation to irony, the intellectualizing, psychologizing, literary radicalization of our mental and artistic life. Gottfried Benn, the Expressionist poet, saw the quintessence of Nietzsche in the statement "fanatics of *expression* 'at any price'" (*BGE*, 197), which according to Benn had led to a language that can desire and accomplish nothing but to scintillate, demonize, and anesthetize. Nietzsche's impact in Europe was widespread and extended from the Russian Symbolists, including Vyacheslav Ivanov, Andrei Belyi, and Valeri Bryusov, to such diverse

authors as August Strindberg, Georg Brandes, William Butler
Yeats, Gabriele d'Annunzio, Robert Musil, and Hermann
Hesse. Gustav Mahler, Frederick Delius, and Richard Strauss
responded musically to Nietzsche, and George Bernard Shaw
brought the *Übermensch*, as the "superman," to the London
stage in 1903.

In contrast to this many-sided literary reception, the reception of Nietzsche within the discipline of philosophy was sur-
prisingly narrow and provincial. Wilhelm Dilthey, Nietzsche's
contemporary, mentioned Nietzsche for the first time in 1898
and portrayed him as an opponent of historical consciousness,
someone who had written "his denunciation of history" in
Basel and, "in the ongoing torture of his brooding over himself" or in subjective introspection, had tried to reach self-
understanding.[1] Dilthey expanded his image in later writings
but never really understood the powerful fascination of Nietzsche's thought. Nietzsche was relegated to the philosophy of
life, or vitalistic *Lebensphilosophie*, a project in which Dilthey
himself was involved. During the first decades of the twentieth
century, he was classified together with Georg Simmel, Ludwig Klages, Henri Bergson, and others. For Dilthey this was a
philosophical movement attempting "to interpret the world on
its own terms" and required an empathetic approach to the
world, a type of recognition achieved by projecting oneself into
the object "as the interpreter relates to a work of art." The
"interpretation of the world on its own terms" became, according to Dilthey, "the motto of all free spirits" over the course of
the nineteenth century. Following the decline of the Hegelian
system, it was developed further by Schopenhauer, Feuerbach,
Richard Wagner, and Nietzsche.[2] Heidegger mentions the interpretation of Nietzsche as a philosopher of life somewhat

[1] Wilhelm Dilthey, *Die Jugendgeschichte Hegels und andere Abhandlungen
zur Geschichte des deutschen Idealismus*, ed. Hermann Nohl, in Wilhelm Dilthey, *Gesammelte Schriften* (Göttingen: Vandenhoeck und Ruprecht, 1959),
4: 528–29.

[2] Ibid., 4: 210–11.

disdainfully at the beginning of his lectures (*N*, 1: 5). By contrast, Heidegger wants to show "that Nietzsche moves in the orbit of the question of Western philosophy" and that Nietzsche knew what it meant "to be at home in genuine questioning" (*N*, 1: 4, 6).

Here Heidegger virtually ignores two prominent contemporary interpreters: Karl Jaspers and Max Scheler. He does not mention Scheler once, and he rejects Jaspers's approach, arguing that Jaspers is unable to see teachings like the eternal recurrence of the same "as a question of great import, because, according to Jaspers, there is no conceptual truth or conceptual knowledge in philosophy" (*N*, 1: 23). Yet these philosophers had displaced the literary and poetic reception of Nietzsche in favor of his philosophical concepts: Scheler, through the analyses of competition, efficiency, success, human idols, and the value-producing power of *ressentiment*.[3] Jaspers, who is more widely known in English, had drawn attention to Nietzsche's persistent questioning of every self-enclosed form of rationality as a particular feature and previously unrealized kind of modernity in his philosophizing. This is the thrust of Jaspers's analyses of Nietzsche's "philosophical activity" in terms of infinite reflection, masks, self-dissembling writing, groundless thought, and an infinitely self-completing dialectic that brings all apodictic statements into question through the consideration of new possibilities.[4]

In *Vernunft und Existenz* (Reason and existence) from 1935, Jaspers had tried to integrate these aspects of Nietzsche's thought into his own philosophy of existence. In the famous

[3]Max Scheler, *Das Ressentiment im Aufbau der Moralen*, in idem, *Gesammelte Werke*, vol. 3, *Vom Umsturz der Werte* (Bern: Francke, 1955), 33–147.

[4]Karl Jaspers, *Nietzsche: An Introduction to the Understanding of His Philosophical Activity*, trans. Charles F. Wallraff and Frederick J. Schmitz (South Bend, Ind.: Regnery/Gateway, 1979); Karl Jaspers, *Nietzsche und das Christentum* (Hameln: Bücherstube Fritz Seifert, 1938).

introduction to this text, Jaspers portrayed Nietzsche's and
Kierkegaard's work as prime examples of two important arguments against the basic tendency of Western thought to
transform everything non-rational or counter-rational into rationality and to ground reason on its own basis.[5] To illustrate
this thesis, Jaspers divided the intellectual history of the West
into: (1) a period marked by the domination of the *logos* and
the admonition "Know thyself," which culminated in Hegel,
and (2) a period characterized by a radical disillusionment with
the self-confidence of reason, the dissolution of all boundaries,
and the collapse of all authority, a period that begins with Kierkegaard and Nietzsche. With their claim that human knowledge is nothing but interpretation, their seductive willingness
to indulge in concealment and masks, and their dizzying call
for a truthfulness that continually calls itself into question, they
represent "modernity somersaulting over itself." They offer
"no teachings, no basic position, not a worldview, but a new,
basic manner of thinking of people in the medium of infinite
reflection, a reflection conscious that, as reflection, it can no
longer gain a foundation." We know that Nietzsche had seen
Dostoyevsky as his nearest relative, particularly in regards to
the "Notes from Underground," which he had characterized
as "a kind of self-parody of the *gnothi sauton*" (need to know
oneself).[6]

For Heidegger, however, all these approaches were irrele-
vant to the interpretation of Nietzsche. He wanted to read
Nietzsche's philosophy as an answer to the guiding question
of philosophy, "What is Being?," and to provide evidence
"that Nietzsche knew what philosophy is" (*N*, 1: 4). A more
direct connection exists between Heidegger's Nietzsche and
the Nietzsche presented in Karl Löwith's book *Nietzsche's Philosophy of the Eternal Recurrence of the Same*; the first edition
of this appeared in 1934 but at the time went largely unno-

[5]See Karl Jaspers, *Vernunft und Existenz* (Munich: Piper, 1973).
[6]Nietzsche to Overbeck, Feb. 23, 1887, in *KGB*, 5: 27–28.

ticed.[7] Löwith, too, concentrated on Nietzsche's "philosophical doctrine," in contrast to all those who had written on Nietzsche *and* some other topic, such as Romanticism (Karl Joël), Nietzsche's "psychological accomplishments" (Ludwig Klages), Schopenhauer (Georg Simmel), or politics (Alfred Bäumler). Löwith assumed, as Heidegger did, that the task of the philosopher was to bring to light a central thought as the organizing principle of philosophy. To Löwith the structural principle of Nietzsche's thought was the doctrine of the eternal recurrence of the same, and this raised Nietzsche, Löwith believed, from a mere cultural critic and writer of aphorisms to a true philosopher.

But Löwith also asked himself "whether Heidegger had perceived Nietzsche's doctrine as Nietzsche had himself, namely, as the primal law of all *living beings*" (222). Heidegger's readings of Nietzsche seemed to Löwith too restrictive, limited to a posited history of Being in a particular epoch. At the end of the essay "Who Is Nietzsche's Zarathustra?," for example, Heidegger interprets the essence of modern technology, the "power-driven machine," as an "offshoot of the eternal recurrence of the same" (*N*, 2: 233).[8] For Löwith, however, this doctrine was Nietzsche's attempt "to translate people, who have become de-centered, back into the eternal 'grounding text of nature'" (223). At the end of his summary "On the History of Nietzsche Interpretation (1894–1954)," Löwith wrote: "If Nietzsche had thought of what is obviously happening 'now,' in the age of the will to power and the coming organization of the earth, he would have remained an 'untimely' critic of his time. Since he freed himself from the sickness of the time, however, he became one

---

[7]Karl Löwith, *Nietzsches Philosophie der ewigen Wiederkehr des Gleichen* (Stuttgart: Kohlhammer, 1956). Page numbers of quotations from this work are given in the text.

[8]"Who Is Nietzsche's Zarathustra?" was a lecture delivered to the Bremen Club on May 8, 1953; for an English translation, see *N*, 2: 209–33.

of 'the edifying ones,' one of those last lovers of wisdom who knew about the eternal becoming that always recurs and remains the same throughout all the changes and transformations of beings" (225). Heidegger went far beyond such an argument. First, he decided that Nietzsche's central thought was not actually present in his writings, or present only in an unthought, unelaborated way, but had to be realized through our efforts, through hermeneutics and "a better understanding." In order to accomplish this realization, a double effort is necessary: we must intensively fuse together the apparently irreconcilable concepts of the will to power and the eternal recurrence of the same, so that they are seen as two aspects of one and the same concept. In classical terminology, the will to power is the essence (*essentia*) of all things, whereas the eternal recurrence of the same is its existence (*existentia*). In the language of transcendental philosophy, the will to power is the thing in itself (*noumenon*), and the eternal recurrence of the same is appearance (*phainomenon*). In Heidegger's terminology of "the ontic-ontological difference," which refers to the fundamental difference between Being and beings, the will to power in Nietzsche's metaphysics stands for Being, and the eternal recurrence of the same stands for the multiplicity of beings (*N*, 3: 168).

As Heidegger joined the will to power and the eternal recurrence of the same into one and the same thought, he tried to "complete" Nietzsche's thinking and to end the Western project known as "metaphysics." Heidegger developed this reading over the course of his lectures in several variations and from many different perspectives. The lectures on Nietzsche from the winter semester of 1936–37 demonstrate the unity of the will to power and the eternal recurrence of the same in terms of art and aesthetics, and are entitled "The Will to Power as Art" (1936/37) (*N*, 1: 1–220). The lectures from the summer semester of 1937 proceed in the reverse direction and bear the title "The Eternal Recurrence of the Same" (1937) (*N*, 2:

1–208).[9] During the summer semester of 1939, Heidegger discussed his topic from the perspective of philosophical cognition and entitled the lecture series "The Will to Power as Knowledge" (1939) (*N*, 3: 1–158). As the dates suggest, the texts of these years are closely linked to the political, military, and historical events of the time.

The remaining texts of Heidegger's *Nietzsche* cannot be so easily situated. The next in the series, "The Eternal Recurrence of the Same and the Will to Power" (1939) (*N*, 3: 159–83), thematizes the connections between the two concepts and has the nature of a conclusion. In a footnote to the preceding lecture, Heidegger stated that the presentation of his lectures had been disrupted by the premature close of the semester in July 1939, and he was therefore publishing the text of the two planned concluding lectures separately. He specified that these two lectures "in summary of all that has preceded, attempt to think 'The Will to Power as Art,' 'The Eternal Recurrence of the Same,' and 'The Will to Power as Knowledge' together."[10] As a war measure the semester system was briefly changed into a trimester system. During the second trimester of 1940, Heidegger continued his investigation of the will to power from the important new perspective of "European nihilism," which is also the title of the lecture series (*N*, 4: 1–196).[11] Another text, "Nietzsche's Metaphysics" (*N*, 3: 185–251), was written from August to December 1940, possibly for a lecture course or seminar, although it is uncertain whether this convoluted

[9]Now edited according to the lecture manuscripts: Martin Heidegger, *Gesamtausgabe*, vol. 44, *Nietzsches metaphysische Grundstellung im abendländischen Denken: Die ewige Wiederkehr des Gleichen*, ed. Marion Heinz (Frankfurt: Klostermann, 1986).

[10]These lines appear at the end of the first volume in German: Martin Heidegger, *Nietzsche* (Pfullingen: Neske, 1961), 1: 658.

[11]These lectures have recently appeared in Martin Heidegger, *Gesamtausgabe*, vol. 48, *Nietzsche: Der europäische Nihilismus*, ed. Peter Jäger (Frankfurt: Klostermann, 1986). See esp. the editorial preface to the American translation (*N*, 4: viii–x).

text was ever presented.[12] The last texts from this complex date from the final years of the war and describe the history of the concept of Being and Nietzsche's position in it. "Nihilism as Determined by the History of Being" (1944–46) is the last in this sequence, and its composition coincided with the war's end (*N*, 4: 197–250). The last three essays in the second volume of the edition published by Neske in 1961 ("Metaphysics as History of Being," "Sketches for a History of Being as Metaphysics," and "Recollection of Metaphysics," all from 1941) go beyond Nietzsche and have become prominent in the discussion of the topic of "the end of philosophy." They do not appear in the North American edition of Heidegger's Nietzsche lectures, since they had previously been separated from the complex by Heidegger and his translator Joan Stambaugh and had appeared as a separate volume.[13]

Whereas the lectures, according to Heidegger, were "still under way" at the time and "paved the way for the confrontation," the essays "extend the way" of the lecture courses (*N*, 1: xv). The lectures contain considerable material that leads far beyond Nietzsche and makes broad historical connections. The first lectures on "The Will to Power as Art," for example, present a comprehensive history of aesthetic thought with detailed analyses of the relevant doctrines of Plato and Kant. The third cycle of lectures, "The Will to Power as Knowledge," deals with the history of logic and the Western conception of truth. These texts are critical accounts, organized in terms of Heidegger's distinctive concerns. He considers themes from his perspective of the most essential philosophy (metaphysics), but these texts give the same impression of a certain emptiness or lack of content as his other writings give, even when they concern themselves with concrete, historico-philological materials.

[12]Cf. Krell's introductory remarks (*N*, 3: viii).

[13]Martin Heidegger, *The End of Philosophy*, trans. Joan Stambaugh (New York: Harper & Row, 1973).

The situation of the texts has changed in the meantime; since 1986 Heidegger's Nietzsche lectures have begun to appear in the *Gesamtausgabe (Collected Works)*. These texts are based on the original manuscripts, or rather transcripts of the manuscripts, and are closer to the original lectures. The texts of two lecture courses have so far appeared: "Nietzsches metaphysische Grundstellung im abendländischen Denken: Die ewige Wiederkehr des Gleichen" ("Nietzsche's metaphysical position in Western thought. The eternal recurrence of the same," summer semester 1937) and "Nietzsche: Der europäische Nihilismus" ("Nietzsche: European nihilism," second trimester 1940). When Heidegger first published the lectures in 1961, he held to the original text even if it had, as part of its character as a lecture, "an unavoidable breadth of presentation and a certain amount of repetition" (*N*, 1: xv). But he eliminated the arrangement according to lecture hours, subtitled the texts, ordered them by theme, condensed them, and composed them more rigorously. Two essays from this cycle, "The Word of Nietzsche: 'God Is Dead'" (1943) and "Who Is Nietzsche's Zarathustra?" (1953), were taken a step further and disconnected somewhat from the lectures; they represent distinct writings in Heidegger's characteristic manner.[14]

These are the texts of Heidegger's *Nietzsche* that arose from 1936 to 1946, a time of apocalyptic events in Germany. In those years Heidegger achieved a new understanding not only of Nietzsche's thought but also of his own philosophical position. "The question of Being," which dominated his thinking, evolved from the systematic, transcendental-philosophical, phenomenological, or hermeneutic "analysis of Dasein" to a "history of Being," that is, a history of the interpretation of Being over the course of Western metaphysics. Plato, who began this history, and Nietzsche, who ended it, were the two pillars of Western metaphysics. The rapid, catastrophic col-

---

[14]"The Word of Nietzsche: 'God Is Dead'" appears in English in *QT*, 53–112. For "Who Is Nietzsche's Zarathustra?," see note 8 to this chapter.

lapse of Hitler's Reich, the articulation of the will to power as
the basic thought of Nietzsche's philosophy, and the conclusion
of Western metaphysics in Heidegger's history of Being con-
verged at this point in a unique and unsettling way.
Heidegger published only two lectures during the war
years: "Plato's Doctrine of Truth" (1942) and "On the Essence
of Truth" (1943), which were written in 1930 and 1931, respectively. His *Erläuterungen zu Hölderlins Dichtung* (1951) contains treatises and various lectures from 1936 to 1943 that have
some bearing on his philosophical development at this time (*N*,
1: xvi). When he reappeared as a philosopher after World War
II with the *Letter on Humanism* of 1947, the lectures and notes
on Nietzsche were the most important documentation on the
path that Heidegger had followed since 1930. They were
treated as a central work by the author when he published the
texts in 1961. A further text belonging to this sequence of writings is the essay "Overcoming Metaphysics" of 1951, which also
returns to the complex of Nietzsche's texts from 1936 to 1946.[15]
Taken together, Heidegger's texts on Nietzsche and the history
of Being or the end of philosophy have a reciprocal relationship
to each other.
The texts on Nietzsche, which occupied Heidegger for
more than ten years, in no way represent a unified position
with a coherent interpretation. As I have suggested, Heidegger
changed his perspective constantly: at one point he would take
the self-propagating thought of the subject and generally in-
tensifying subjectivism as his opening, at another point he
would highlight the domination of the philosophy of value,
and at still a third point he would consider the progressive
nihilism of the Western tradition.
The central issue in all these divergent approaches is, however, Heidegger's "ontic-ontological difference," the distinc-

[15]Martin Heidegger, "Überwindung der Metaphysik," in idem, *Vorträge
und Aufsätze* (Pfullingen: Neske, 1954), 71–100. For an English translation
of this essay, see *The End of Philosophy* (cited in note 13 to this chapter). See
also D. F. Krell's remarks, *N*, 4: x.

tion between Being and beings (*ontōs on*, Being of beings) in Western metaphysics. As is well known, the distinction is deeply problematic for Heidegger because the concept of Being that results from this presupposition is so abstract that only the most general things can be said about it (*N*, 4: 157). Being enters into such a limitless process of forgetting "that its very forgottenness is sucked into its own vortex" (*N*, 4: 193). Throughout his various approaches to Nietzsche and to the European history of Being, Heidegger elaborates his underlying dismay or bewilderment in the face of this event, which he had already formulated in *Being and Time*: "In the history of Western thought, from its inception, the Being of beings has indeed been thought, but the truth of Being as Being remains unthought; not only is such truth denied as a possible experience for thinking, but Western thought, as metaphysics, expressly though unwittingly conceals the occurrence of this refusal" (*N*, 3: 189–90). In order not to conceal this refusal from ourselves, we would have to admit "that the foundations on which one continues to build one form of metaphysics after another *are no foundations at all*" (*N*, 4: 163).

Nor could Heidegger find in Nietzsche the question of the truth of Being, for it had been concealed, resisted, or, in a manner known only to Heidegger, formulated as a question of the Being of beings and answered with the will to power. In the essay "The Word of Nietzsche: 'God Is Dead,' " Heidegger pays special attention to the critical, destructive character of Nietzsche's writing expressed most prominently in the theme of the death of God. This assessment is also, for Heidegger, the most concise and most consequential summary of the meaninglessness of previous Western metaphysics. According to Heidegger, Nietzsche revealed the meaninglessness of this event but was unable to bring himself out of it. The opening he had created was immediately blocked by the acceptance of the will to power and the eternal recurrence of the same. These prevented him from uncovering the truth of Being. Despite all his revaluations of metaphysics, Nietzsche therefore remained "in the unbroken path of the tradition." With the interpretation of Being as will to power, however, Nietzsche realized the most extreme possibility of philosophy. He had inverted Platonism, which for Heidegger represented the essence of traditional metaphysics, although this reversal remained metaphysical as a form of inverse Platonism. As metaphysics, philosophy had entered its last phase and had spoken its last word.[16] Heidegger's lectures on Nietzsche are his most direct and most comprehensive statement of the "history of Being as metaphysics" and develop these thoughts for the first time in a coherent way.[17] The project of such a history goes back to *Being and Time*, where it is outlined under the title "The Task of Destroying the History of Ontology" and described as the project of the destruction of metaphysics.[18] Despite his preference for words of German origin, Heidegger did not use the term *Zerstörung* but the more Latinate *Destruktion*. He understood this in the sense not of destruction or annihilation, as in the Latinate languages, but of demolition, dismemberment, or taking apart, the *de-struere* of those sedimented layers and residual accretions that have hidden the original nature of Being over the course of intellectual history and were accumulated by metaphysical thinking. In this sense the Heideggerian project of a "destruction of metaphysics" is directly related to Derrida's "deconstruction of metaphysics and logocentrism." It can even be said that Derrida, through the insertion of the syllable *con* in the Heideggerian "destruction" has, at least in the

[16]See Heidegger, "The Word of Nietzsche: 'God Is Dead'"; and idem, "Who Is Nietzsche's Zarathustra?" (cited in notes 14 and 8, respectively, to this chapter).

[17]See Stambaugh's introduction to Heidegger, *The End of Philosophy* (cited in note 13 to this chapter), vii; and Otto Pöggeler, *Der Denkweg Martin Heideggers* (Pfullingen: Neske, 1963), 135–42.

[18]*BAT*, 41–49.

French language and fortuitously in English, more clearly expressed Heidegger's intended meaning.[19]

Of course, Derrida's deconstruction unfolds in terms of formal, semiological functions, above all in terms of writing. In contrast to this synchronic procedure, Heidegger's destruction of metaphysics proceeds diachronically and narrates the history of Being. But Heidegger's project was initially conceived as the phenomenological, transcendental, or hermeneutic analysis of Dasein. The project changed in the "turn" (*Kehre*) that took place over the course of the lectures on Nietzsche because phenomenology, transcendentalism, and hermeneutics also belong to the history of ontology and thus are not in a position to destroy or to overcome this history.[20]

The transformation from the destruction of metaphysics to a history of Being had important consequences for Heidegger's concept of the forgottenness of Being. In this regard it is also of great significance for his image of Nietzsche. Whereas the concealment and the subsequent forgottenness of Being were originally the result of a reductionist naming of Being as idea, cogito, subjectivity, will, and so on, the concept of the history of Being suggests that Being would like to achieve expression in the concepts of the thinker, that Being has entrusted itself to certain thinkers, and that these thinkers "utter Being, that is, utter *the Being of beings* within metaphysics" (*N*, 3: 188). Being withdraws and conceals itself under their words. The forgottenness of Being is no longer simply a slip of the tongue, as in the statement "I have forgotten my umbrella," but belongs to the essence of Being and controls its destiny.[21]

Systematic coherence is thus only one aspect of Heidegger's

[19]On this point, cf. Jacques Derrida, *Psyché* (Paris: Galilée, 1987), 387–93.

[20]See Stambaugh's introduction to Martin Heidegger, *The End of Philosophy* (cited in note 13 to this chapter), ix.

[21]Martin Heidegger, "Zur Seinsfrage," in idem, *Wegmarken* (Frankfurt: Klostermann, 1967), 243. For an English-German bilingual version of this text, see *QB*.

Nietzsche, only the "proximate goal" of his interpretation, though it is necessary to uncover the world-historical dimensions of this philosophy. This becomes, in effect, the "farthest goal" of Heidegger's interpretation (*N*, 3: 190–91). In 1881 or 1882 Nietzsche wrote in his notebook: "The time is coming when the struggle for world domination will be carried on—it will be carried on in the name of *fundamental philosophical doctrines*" (*N*, 3: 190). Heidegger's "proximate goal" was to reconstruct these fundamental philosophical doctrines—which would ultimately determine the struggle for world domination—from Nietzsche's aphoristic and fragmentary text and to uncover their "hidden unity," however incoherently and obliquely Nietzsche may have formulated them. These doctrines emerge from Nietzsche's text in a "unique sequence and manner," but no one had yet addressed the question of which sequence and according to which "essential unity." For Heidegger, in any case: "The hidden unity of the 'fundamental philosophical doctrines' constitutes the essential junctures of Nietzsche's metaphysics. On the basis of this metaphysics, and according to the direction it takes, the consummation of the modern age unfolds its history. Presumably, it will be a long history" (*N*, 3: 190).

The "farthest goal" of the Heideggerian interpretation follows from the attempt to bring "the dawning age" to consciousness, "without reservation and without obfuscation" of the fundamental doctrines for which "the struggle for world domination will be carried out" (*N*, 3: 190). Once these doctrines have been revealed, the struggle can be conducted "on the basis of supreme *consciousness*. For the latter corresponds to the Being that sustains and governs our age" (*N*, 3: 190). This struggle and "the unfolding of the metaphysics that sustains it" mark the "fulfillment of an era of world history and of historical mankind" (*N*, 3: 190–91). Nietzsche thus achieved the "consummation of the age of Western metaphysics" that is the "epoch" inaugurated by Plato. The epoch culminates in the struggle for world domination in the name of Nietzsche's fundamental doctrines, or more precisely, in the name of Heidegger's construal of Nietzsche's fundamental doctrines. What occurs after this "struggle for power on earth" is a "fundamental historical situation" of an entirely different kind. It is no longer a struggle or contest "to master beings," but a "confrontation between the power of beings and the truth of Being" (*N*, 3: 191). In "Nietzsche's Metaphysics" from 1940, Heidegger states that the "farthest goal," the truth of Being, "remains infinitely far from the demonstrable events and circumstances of the present age" and "belongs to the historical remoteness of another history" (*N*, 3: 191). Insofar as humans within contemporary history "belong to Being and its truth," however, this farthest goal is at the same time very near, "nearer than what is otherwise near and the nearest," "primordial," and has its most primordial function as "poetic creation in the sense of poetry" (*N*, 3: 191).

These arguments exemplify Heidegger's oscillating image of the end of metaphysics and the transition to the question of the truth of Being. He clarifies this transition by emphasizing that the "talk of the end of metaphysics" does not mean "that in the future men will no longer 'live' who think metaphysically and generate 'systems of metaphysics'" (*N*, 4: 148). Rather, the image of the end of metaphysics describes a transitional phase leading to its "resurrection in altered forms," an alteration that will be fundamental since we have no names for this process and can have no image of it. In this transitional period, the old "fundamental metaphysical positions" should take over "the purely economic role of providing raw materials with which—once they are correspondingly transformed—the world of 'knowledge' is built 'anew'" (*N*, 4: 148). At any rate it can be assumed that the "historical moment" has occurred "in which *the essential possibilities of metaphysics* are exhausted" (*N*, 4: 148). The "likely" way of thinking at the beginning of the transitional phase is "in terms of various fundamental metaphysical positions and their individual doctrines and concepts," for example, the *"anthropological* mode of thinking" evident in the agreement of philosophical discourses during the postwar years on the "unity of human reality" or the "worldview" (*N*, 4: 149). In the writings of the late Heidegger, this period is characterized by infinite emptiness or universal hopelessness and designated as the "American age" of cybernetics and the computer,[22] the age of "anything goes," the age for which Jean-François Lyotard has established the concept of postmodernity.[23] Yet even in these bleak images of the end of Western philosophy, Heidegger's thinking remains historically and structurally oriented toward a clearing, toward the truth of Being, just as his understanding of Nietzsche as "the end of Western metaphysics" is determined by the "question of the truth of Being" (*N*, 1: 10).

For my purposes the history of Being prior to Nietzsche is less significant, though Heidegger repeatedly tells this story with only slight variations. The main figures include Plato, who interpreted Being as "idea"; Descartes and Kant, who transformed "idea" into "perception" and "transcendental subjectivity" into "the condition for the possibility of beings"; and finally Hegel and Nietzsche, who analyzed the concept of human subjectivity (*animal rationale*) and divided it into two constituents: from Hegel came the elevation of *rationalitas* to speculative-dialectical form as the decisive principle; from Nietzsche came the notion of *brutalitas* and *bestialitas* as the unconditioned essence of subjectivity (*N*, 4: 147–48). Thus Nietzsche, at the end of metaphysics, realized that *"Homo est brutum bestiale"* (The human is a bestial brute; *N*, 4: 148). For Heidegger, this means that "Nietzsche's phrase about the

---

[22]For Heidegger's view of "Americanism," see idem, "The Age of the World Picture" (*QT*, 115–54, esp. 153, note 12). For his view of cybernetics, see idem, "The End of Philosophy and the Task of Thinking," in *OTB*, 55–73, esp. 58–59.

[23]Jean-François Lyotard, *The Postmodern Condition: A Report on Knowledge*, trans. Geoff Bennington and Brian Massumi (Minneapolis: University of Minnesota Press, 1984).

'blond beast'" was in no way "a casual exaggeration, but the password and countersign for a context in which he consciously stood, without being able to peer through its essential historical connections" (*N*, 4: 148). Nietzsche uncovered the consequences of metaphysics that had been valid for Plato but had remained hidden from him (*N*, 4: 205).

It is fitting for this "history" of Being—a narrative that covers nearly two thousand years in only a few moments, gradually empties of all content, and operates quite schematically—that the truths formulated during its progress were articulated neither by individual persons nor by the discursive formations of specific historical periods. They are of anonymous provenance. Of course metaphysics is personal and bound to history, but only in an external sense and as an "aftereffect" (*N*, 3: 188). For Heidegger, a thinker is above all "someone who is called upon to preserve truth in thought," and who will indicate and prepare "a place for mankind within the history of truth" (*N*, 3: 188). The positions represented by individual thinkers within the history of metaphysics are therefore not "the accomplishment and property or even the personal distinction of these thinkers as personalities engaged in a cultural activity" (*N*, 3: 188). Instead, "these thinkers are what they are insofar as the truth of Being has been entrusted to them in such a way that they utter Being, that is, utter *the Being of beings* within metaphysics" (*N*, 3: 188). The metaphysical distinction between Being and beings does not arise from "the thought process of the thinker, but from the essence of the history in which he himself is thinking and in which he is and has to be" (*N*, 4: 182). Fundamental metaphysical experiences belong neither to the thinker's "educational background" (*N*, 4: 181), nor to the historico-biographical or anthropologico-psychological existence of these thinkers; rather, they take place "in terms of Being's essentially occurring truth," in whose domain these thinkers become "exclusively constituted" (*N*, 4: 181).

With this we reach, according to Heidegger, the "most concealed history of Being," for which we are "ill-prepared" (*N*,

4: 178). Although the description of this process is intended as an historical meditation on the history of the truth of beings, these comments typically provide an "historiological report of various interpretations of the Being of beings" (*N*, 4: 178). Truth, the truth of beings, the determination of the Being of beings as the truth of beings, is "historical in its own Being" and "always demands a humankind through which it is enjoined, grounded, communicated, and thus safeguarded" (*N*, 3: 187). This is the case not "because being human elapses in the course of time" but because "mankind is transposed or sent into metaphysics, and because metaphysics alone is able to ground an epoch insofar as it establishes and *maintains* humankind in a truth concerning beings as such and as a whole" (*N*, 3: 187). In "Recollection in Metaphysics" (1941), Heidegger went so far as to separate entirely the history of Being from human history: "The history of Being is neither the history of man and of humanity, nor the history of the human relation to beings and to Being. The history of Being is Being itself, and only Being" (*EP*, 75–83, 82). The human being becomes involved in this history "only with regard to the manner in which he takes his essence from the relation of Being to himself and, in accordance with this relation, loses his essence, neglects it, gives it up, grounds it, or squanders it" (*EP*, 82).

According to Heidegger, this was the way that Nietzsche's metaphysics of the will to power arose. At about the time when Nietzsche was writing *Daybreak* (1881), "a light dawns over Nietzsche's metaphysical path" (*N*, 3: 188). For almost ten years, Nietzsche "wends his way in the most luminous brightness of this experience" (*N*, 3: 188). During these years, "the truth of beings as such and as a whole seeks to come to expression in his thought" (*N*, 3: 188). Plans, sketches, attempts, and alterations from this time are not "signs," not "programs" of something uncompleted, "but records in which unmooted yet unmistakable paths are preserved, paths along which Nietzsche had to wander in the realm of the truth of beings as such" (*N*, 3: 189). Heidegger states explicitly: "That the Being of

beings becomes operative as will to power is not the result of
the emergence of Nietzsche's metaphysics. Rather, Nietzsche's
thought has to plunge into metaphysics because Being radiates
its own essence as will to power; that is, as the sort of thing that
in the history of the truth of beings must be grasped through
the projection as will to power" (*N*, 4: 181).

Heidegger's *Nietzsche* combines systematic interpretation
(the will to power and eternal recurrence of the same) with the
history of metaphysics (the culmination of Western metaphysics) into the most coherent interpretation of Nietzsche yet. In
fact, Heidegger's oscillations emerge clearly from this perspective, since the complete system is nowhere presented in its entirety but is deployed variously from new perspectives within
the ten sections of the volumes of his *Nietzsche* and can be
unified only through a reductive reading. The individual sections represent a considerable period of time in Heidegger's
intellectual development, his "pathway of thinking" (Pöggeler), and in addition encompass years marked by the most concentrated series of events in modern history. Heidegger's
Nietzsche cannot, therefore, be reduced to individual statements; it points ahead again and again, in the shifting scenes
of the text, to another version.

Of course, a reader like Derrida is well aware of the complex textuality of this writing. In order to gain a sense of Heidegger's claims, which Derrida treats in equally shifting ways
and criticizes from many perspectives, it is useful to consider
at least one section of these texts, a section in which Heidegger
systematizes Nietzsche in exemplary fashion from one perspective. Heidegger's interpretation is by no means exhausted
by this one example, but from among the ten sections there is
probably no better point of entry into his reading than the 1940
essay "Nietzsche's Metaphysics." In this text the notion of
metaphysics as "the truth of the Being of beings" remains in
the foreground. Nietzsche's metaphysics are treated as an
amalgam of five concepts, in which each of the last four necessarily arises from the preceding one.

According to Heidegger, when Nietzsche characterized the essence of all beings as will to power (first concept), he reached this point not on the basis of a romantic drive for power or a mean lust for cruelty but through "the innermost essence of Being," "the basic character of beings as such" (*N*, 3: 193). The "conjunction of the words" *will to power* was itself unusual for this kind of attempt; Heidegger mentions this to show that Nietzsche's thinking remains the most thoroughly consequential of all metaphysics. It would have been insufficient to ground this thinking in the constitution of individual beings, as if it involved merely a particular attitude toward life. On the fundamental level of the most essential form of philosophy, the will to power involves mastering every phase of power as a continual "enhancement of power," "the animation—holding sway on its own terms—of the will" (*N*, 3: 197). Hence the will to power governs all "value estimating"—that is, both valuation and value thinking (*N*, 3: 199–200).

The next step is nihilism (second concept), which for Heidegger follows necessarily from the first. At the beginning of metaphysics, with Plato, the idea and the concept of the good did not yet have the character of values. For Nietzsche, however, all philosophy since Plato is a metaphysics of values. True being—God, the Christian Redeemer, the moral law, the authority of reason, progress, the happiness of the greatest number—became a metaphysics of values, wishes, and ideals. But from the perspective of the will to power, Nietzsche found that all these earlier values have been devalued. This devaluation is expressed in his assertion that "God is dead," which indicates that such ideals have lost "their capacity to shape history" (*N*, 3: 203). Nihilism becomes a fundamental event of Western history, since it marks the necessary completion of Western metaphysics, "the lawfulness of this historic occurrence, its 'logic'" (*N*, 3: 205). But nihilism does not "strive for mere nullity" (*N*, 3: 204); it seeks to establish new values as "the ideal of the *supreme degree of powerfulness* of spirit" (*N*, 3: 208).

If we are looking for a "metaphysical expression" for the

"*way in which* the whole of beings comes to presence," its formulation would be Nietzsche's third concept, "the eternal recurrence of the same" (*N*, 3: 209). Heidegger argues that in the context of Nietzsche's metaphysics the "beingness of beings," "the will to power," "the entirety of beings," and "the eternal recurrence of the same" each evoke in turn the "form of their particular essence" from "the unity of the truth of being" (*N*, 3: 210). The will to power can neither stand still nor grow into infinity; it must therefore culminate in the eternal recurrence of the same (*N*, 3: 211–12). The eternal recurrence, on the other hand, as "the most constant permanentizing of the unstable" (*N*, 3: 212), requires the will to power.

With similar consequences, the person who in any given historical situation is able to think of Being as such as will to power and of Being as a whole as the eternal recurrence of the same is named by Nietzsche's fourth concept, "the overman," known in German as the *Übermensch* (*N*, 3: 216). The will to power brings modern, unconditional subjectivity to its necessary completion with the "reversal of the earlier preeminence of reason into the preeminence of animality" (*N*, 3: 223): "Will to power is therefore both absolute and—because inverted— consummate subjectivity. Such consummation at the same time exhausts the essence of absoluteness" (*N*, 3: 225). Heidegger describes the emergence of the *Übermensch* with insistence: "*The consummate subjectivity of will to power is the metaphysical origin of the essential necessity of the 'overman'*" (*N*, 3: 225).

But the "overman," or *Übermensch*, comes into existence only when the will to power wills it, when "at its zenith will to power itself wills its own essence and thus is concordant with beings as a whole" (*N*, 3: 227). Heidegger speaks in this connection of a new caste, a new race, a new "breed" of human, who gives shape to, breeds, and trains itself. The unique feature of this self-creation and self-breeding is "the straightforward and rigorous simplification of all things and men into a unity, a unity that absolutely empowers the essence of power for *dominion over the earth*" (*N*, 3: 230). Two practices are shaping the struggle for world domination: the "total 'mechanization' of things and the breeding of human beings" (*N*, 3: 230).

Heidegger cites an aphorism of Nietzsche's from "The Wanderer and His Shadow," which describes the "machine" as "a model for party organizations and the conduct of war" and views "the sciences," as "the industrially organized and controlled investigation of all beings," among technologies that serve "the securing of permanence of will to power" (*N*, 3: 230).

The breeding of human beings, he explains, is not "taming in the sense of a suppression and hobbling of sensuality; rather, breeding is the accumulation and purification of energies in the univocality of the strictly controllable 'automatism' of every activity" (*N*, 3: 231). He explains further: "Only where the absolute subjectivity of will to power comes to be the truth of beings as a whole is the *principle* of a program of racial breeding possible; possible, that is, not merely on the basis of naturally evolving races, but in terms of the self-conscious *thought* of race. That is to say, the principle is metaphysically necessary" (*N*, 3: 231). According to Heidegger, it is important to assume that "Nietzsche's thought of will to power was ontological rather than biological" (*N*, 3: 231). From this perspective, Nietzsche's racial thought is "metaphysical rather than biological in meaning" (*N*, 3: 231).

When Heidegger speaks of consummated subjectivity, the breeding of human beings, the simplification of all people and things into a controllable unity, total mechanization, industrial organization, and automation, he usually interprets these phenomena as the climax of the forgottenness of Being. In the summer of 1940, however, at the high point of Hitler's Reich and shortly after the subjugation of France, the situation must have looked different for Heidegger, since he saw all these features as character traits of the "grand style" in the struggle for world domination and described this "grand style" as the "unique determination" of the *Übermensch* (*N*, 3: 232–33). He concludes his striking portrait of the figure with a disturbing

rhapsody to the hammer: "The overman is that casting of mankind which first of all *wills* itself as a casting and even casts
itself as such casting. But to do this, overman requires a 'hammer' with which the casting be struck and tempered, and with
which everything previous, because it is inappropriate to the
overman, be shattered" (*N*, 3: 233).

In light of the four "fundamental expressions," it is not surprising that Nietzsche's fifth concept, "justice," has for Heidegger nothing to do with notions "that derive from Christian,
humanistic, Enlightenment, bourgeois, and socialist morali-
ties" (*N*, 3: 243–44). Instead, it is the concern of "that sort of
mankind which is to be forged and bred into a type, a type that
possesses an essential aptitude for establishing absolute dominion over the earth," the aptitude of the *Übermensch* (*N*, 3: 245).

At this point the question may arise of how to judge Heidegger's frequently discussed relation to National Socialism
from the standpoint of his assessment of Nietzsche as well as
from the perspective of the history of Being. The recent vehement debate over this topic will not be addressed in detail
here.[24] It suffices to consider the positions taken by Richard
Rorty and Jürgen Habermas in this controversy. Rorty, with a
rhetorical shrug of his shoulders, argues "that one of the century's most original thinkers happened to be a pretty nasty
character," someone who denounced his Jewish colleagues behind their backs to the officials and who tried to destroy academic careers on political grounds (*CIS*, 111). By contrast, Habermas, in *The Philosophical Discourse of Modernity*, sees a
direct connection between "the temporalized *philosophy of origins*," the history of Being, and Heidegger's National Socialism (*DM*, 155). Rorty argues that "if one holds [my] view of

---

[24]For the recent state of the discussion and documentation, see Thomas
Sheehan, "Heidegger and the Nazis," *New York Review of Books* 35, 10 (June
1988): 38–47, whose judgment I gladly accept and whose excellent arrangement of the materials I gratefully borrow. Sheehan's evaluation of Heidegger
is essentially: "first, that he remains one of the century's most influential
philosophers and, second, that he was a Nazi" (38).

the self as centerless . . . one will be prepared to find the relation between the intellectual and the moral virtues, and the relation between a writer's books and the other parts of his life, contingent" (*CIS*, 111). Rorty suggests that we should expect just as little connection between the intellectual and personal qualities of a Heidegger as we would of an artist, for example, Richard Wagner. For Rorty, a good portion of Heidegger's later history of Being can be found already in Heidegger's 1927 lectures *The Basic Problems of Phenomenology*.[25] Presumably these would have constituted the second part of *Being and Time*, if Heidegger had ever completed that book. Yet even if the Nazis had not come to power and Heidegger "had never dreamed of becoming Hitler's *éminence grise*," Rorty believes that the "turn" would have occurred (*CIS*, 111).[26]

Habermas, for his part, answers the question of "how fascism played into the very development of Heidegger's theory" (*DM*, 156) by saying that Heidegger needed an excuse for his association with National Socialism, looked for an explanation for his attachment to the movement, and felt compelled to answer the question, as Rorty puts it: "How will I look to history in my Nazi uniform?"[27] In 1933, according to Habermas, Heidegger gave the basic concepts of fundamental ontology "a new content" (*DM*, 157). In place of individual existence, the people (*Volk*) appeared "as the locale in which Dasein's authentic capacity to be whole is to be decided" (*DM*, 157), and the "determination of provisional resoluteness" from *Being and Time* was "concretized into the outbreak of a national revolution" (*DM*, 158). With this, Heidegger "had maneuvered himself philosophically into a difficult situation" (*DM*, 158), insofar as

[25]Martin Heidegger, *The Basic Problems of Phenomenology*, trans. Albert Hofstadter (Bloomington: Indiana University Press, 1982).

[26]But cf. Otto Pöggeler, "Den Führer führen? Heidegger und kein Ende," *Philosophische Rundschau* 32 (1985): 26–67.

[27]Rorty, however, sees the origin of Heidegger's history of Being not in this question but in the question: "Will history see me as just one more disciple of Nietzsche's?" (*CIS*, 111).

he had established "an internal and not easily touched up connection between his philosophy and contemporary events"
(*DM*, 159). A revaluation of National Socialism would have
had to renounce "the foundations of the renewed ontology"
(*DM*, 159).

In this situation, Heidegger decided, with the turn to a history of Being, to give up the last remnant of a claim for grounding the "argumentatively performed existential hermeneutics"
from *Being and Time* (*DM*, 154). The "decisionistic resoluteness" becomes "an anonymous dispensation of Being," outfit-
ted with the attribute of an "occurrence of truth" (*DM*, 155).
With the history of Being, in other words, Heidegger "detaches his actions and statements altogether from himself as an
empirical person and attributes them to a fate for which one
cannot be held responsible" (*DM*, 156). From this point on,
Heidegger understood the turn itself not "as the outcome of an
effort of thought to solve problems, the result of a process of
investigation, but always as the objective event of an anonymous overcoming of metaphysics staged by Being itself" (*DM*,
156). This did not interfere with his claim to be a philosopher,
since Heidegger saw himself as having privileged access to
such an occurrence. For Habermas, however, the thought of a
privileged access to the history of Being has so little "plau-
sibility that it cannot be satisfactorily explained in terms of the
internal motifs" (*DM*, 155). Instead, he would attribute its origin to Heidegger's "temporary identification with the National
Socialist movement" (*DM*, 155), as the "result of his historical
experience with National Socialism" (*DM*, 156).

Out of the subjective affinity with this movement grew an
"objective error," a fatality, a fateful step of "significance related to the history of metaphysics" (*DM*, 159). The "untruth
of the movement," about which "his eyes were only gradually
opened," seemed to Heidegger the "objective withholding of
the truth" (*DM*, 159). This reading by Habermas implies an
essential difference between the early philosophy ("existential

interpretation of conscience") and the writings after the turn
("anonymous fate") and rests equally on the assumption that
Heidegger experienced only a "passing identification" with
the Nazis that lasted until about 1935. Although until then
he trusted the "National Socialist revolution" "to enlist the potential of technology in the service of the project of the new
German Dasein," the reconceptualization of technology as
"*Gestell*" ("enframing") signaled Heidegger's turning away
from this expectation, and the coordination of fascism with
Americanism and communism became the symptoms of the
"metaphysical domination of technology" (*DM*, 159–60). Like
Nietzsche's philosophy, fascism then belonged "to the objectively ambiguous phase of the overcoming of metaphysics"
(*DM*, 160).

Rorty's and Habermas's different explanations of the connection between Heidegger's Nazism and his writings have
been adopted by other interpreters in more or less reconstituted form.[28] One position rests on the assumption of an unbroken unity of the early writings (*Being and Time*) and the
later texts (after the "turn") and finds a complete break between Heidegger's person and his texts, between his political
convictions and actions on the one hand and his metaphysics
or critique of metaphysics on the other. To be sure, Rorty states
his position in such an extreme fashion that one might suspect
that he is ironically offering a caricature of postmodern
thought. Chess players and microbiologists are not held responsible for their political affiliations: why should philoso-

[28]From the voluminous literature on this topic, see Otto Pöggeler, *Phi-
losophie und Politik bei Heidegger* (Freiburg: Alber, 1972); Annemarie Geth-
mann-Siefert and Otto Pöggeler, eds., *Heidegger und die praktische Philoso-
phie*, (Frankfurt: Suhrkamp, 1988); Philippe Lacoue-Labarthe, *Heidegger,
Art and Politics: The Fiction of the Political*, trans. Chris Turner (Oxford:
Basil Blackwell, 1990); Hugo Ott, *Martin Heidegger: Unterwegs zu seiner
Biographie* (Frankfurt: Campus, 1988); Terry Eagleton, *The Ideology of the
Aesthetic* (Oxford: Basil Blackwell, 1990).

phers like Heidegger be made to give an account? He was simply a specialist in Plato, Aristotle, Kant, Schelling, and Hegel. The ways in which he transposed his ideas into political reality should teach us that philosophy as such is not to be taken seriously.[29]

Habermas, by contrast, separates the early from the late Heidegger and sees in the later writings, on the basis of an ideological critique, a desperate attempt to justify the temporary connection with the Nazis through a metaphysical construction. This construction would suspend all personal responsibility, identify all occurrences as the anonymous fate of Being, and reduce history in general to the history of metaphysics. Recently the literary-critical writings of Paul de Man have been explained in similar ways, though on a very different level. Because, it is argued, he had written some newspaper articles during his youth in Belgium that were anti-Semitic and sympathetic to the Nazis, de Man had to deny the continuity of history in his later writings and describe the coherent readability of texts as an impossibility. Like the history of Being for Heidegger, deconstruction for de Man became a means of personally mastering the past.

There is, however, a third interpretive possibility that retains the connection between the early and late writings of Heidegger and at the same time relates all the writings to Nazism. It would not mean in any sense that all Heidegger's writings are set equal to Nazism. This would be the most extreme form of such an approach. Heidegger's connection to Nazism could just as well be seen as an "illusion," a self-delusion, which derived from his belief that he had found his "dream of a folk 'religion'" or a new "religion of humanity" realized there; "the course of things" later taught him better. From this perspective, which is represented by Gadamer, it can no longer be said

[29]See Rorty in *New Republic*, Apr. 11, 1988, and the answer by Tzvetan Todorov in *Times Literary Supplement*, June 17–23, 1988.

"that Heidegger's political confusion had nothing to do with his philosophy." Gadamer remarked: "That anyone could be satisfied with this explanation! They did not see how insulting this defense would be to such an important thinker."[30] For Gadamer, Heidegger kept his dream even after the disappointment over the "failing revolution" of the Nazis, "protected" the dream and "kept it silent" until it later reached as far "as the radical discussion of the end of philosophy."

Although Heidegger himself connected his philosophy with Nazi ideology and perhaps even structurally related it to such a framework, his philosophy remains from this perspective uniquely transcendent in relation to historical reality, and this enables us to pay undiminished attention to it. Indeed, only against this background is it possible for us to grasp the strangeness of Heidegger's thought. Gadamer expressed this most impressively in his Freiburg memorial lecture for Heidegger on December 16, 1976, entitled "Being, Spirit, God": "Whoever has been touched by the thought of Martin Heidegger can no longer read the fundamental expressions of metaphysics, as the title of my presentation names them, in the ways of traditional metaphysics," he said at the outset of this text.[31] Gadamer summarized his position in the contemporary debate over Heidegger's Nazism: "Whoever now believes that we no longer need to consider Heidegger has not yet measured how difficult it was and will always remain for anyone to come to terms with him and not to make a fool of themselves if they act superior."

For Derrida, too, it is axiomatic that we cannot avoid reading Heidegger's texts, although Nazism may be inscribed in the interior of this philosophy. To this day, no one has been

[30]Hans-Georg Gadamer, "Heidegger et la pensée nazie," ed. Catherine David, *Le novel observateur*, Jan. 22–28, 1988; Gadamer, "Zurück von Syrakus?" *Frankfurter Allgemeine Zeitung*, Feb. 15, 1988.

[31]Hans-Georg Gadamer, "Sein Geist Gott," in idem, *Heideggers Wege: Studien zum Spätwerk* (Tübingen: Mohr, 1983), 152.

able to reduce Heidegger's overall thought to Nazi ideology. It is much more a question of tracing the Nazi material in his writing that forces us to think and yet at the same time perplexes us, provokes our uneasiness. Of the motifs in Heidegger's writings that have troubled him, Derrida names the questions of authenticity, proximity, and the homeland—the starting point of *Being and Time*—the critique of technology and science, the conception of animality or sexual difference, the voice, the hand, language, the "epoch" or epochality, and particularly the question of questioning itself, the "piety of thought" that Heidegger foregrounded throughout his work. In relation to these topics, Derrida's readings of Heidegger have always been consciously ambivalent and problematic.[32]

Derrida is doubtlessly the most intensive critic of Heidegger among contemporary thinkers, particularly for his conviction that it would be naive, even politically obscurantist, if one believed that Nazism could be held at a distance from a self-confident liberal humanism and a leftist democratism. Among his numerous recent writings on Heidegger, the most prominent ones deal with *Geschlecht*—"that frighteningly polysemic and practically untranslatable word (race, lineage, stock, generation, sex)"—the "hand," and *Geist* ("mind" and "spirit") in Heidegger's writings.[33] In these texts Derrida sets the stage for the pragmatic treatment of such topics in Heidegger and illuminates the interlacing of Heidegger's writings with Nazism. The writing on the *Geist* (*OS*) is of particular interest in this regard, since it deals with the pivotal metaphor of "spirit" in

[32]See Jacques Derrida, "Heidegger, l'enfer des philosophes," interview with Didier Eribon, *Le novel observateur*, Nov. 6–12, 1987.

[33]Jacques Derrida, "Geschlecht: Sexual Difference, Ontological Difference," *Research in Phenomenology* 13 (1983): 65–83; idem, "Geschlecht II: Heidegger's Hand," in *Deconstruction and Philosophy: The Texts of Jacques Derrida*, ed. John Sallis (Chicago: University of Chicago Press, 1987), 161–96. For the French version of these two texts, see Derrida, *Psyché* (Paris: Galilée, 1987). On the translation of "Geschlecht," see *OS*, 7.

Heidegger and appeared just after the publication of the book by Victor Farias that reopened the controversy over Heidegger's Nazism.[34]

In *Being and Time,* Heidegger had decided to avoid the word *Geist* because it blocked the way to the question of Being, but in the notorious Rector's Address of 1933[35] he lifted the quotation marks he had used to cloak the term and Germanized it in the direction of *Gemüt* ("spirit") (*OS*, 21). The spirit then emerged under the sign of leadership (*Führung*) and appeared more assertively in the *Introduction* [*Einführung*] *to Metaphysics* (1953).[36] In 1953, spirit reappeared in Heidegger's reading of Georg Trakl as the self-igniting flame that leaves behind white ashes.[37] Despite the ideological proximity to the Nazi mentality, Heidegger's spirit remained at a distance from the reality of this world. His tortuous strategy in the use of the word *spirit* is understandable if we think of Nazi rhetoric in general, particularly of its biologizing tendencies in accordance with Rosenberg's style. In this way Heidegger sought to extricate himself from his usage of words. Derrida's reading of Paul de Man also tries to establish the undecidability or the ambiguous status of his texts, although these writings—the journalistic, occasional essays of a younger man—are clearly of a much lesser caliber. In regard to the consequences of the young de Man's engagement with Nazism for his later writings, however, Derrida is of the opinion that rejecting them would re-

---

[34]Victor Farias, *Heidegger and Nazism,* ed. Joseph Margolis and Tom Rockmore (Philadelphia: Temple University Press, 1989). For further analysis of both Derrida's and Farias's positions, see Lacoue-Labarthe, *Heidegger, Art and Politics* (cited in note 28 to this chapter), esp. 123–37.

[35]Heidegger, "The Self-Assertion of the German University," trans. Karsten Harries, *Review of Metaphysics* 38, no. 3 (1985): 470–80.

[36]Heidegger, *An Introduction to Metaphysics,* trans. Ralph Manheim (Garden City, N.Y.: Doubleday, Anchor, 1961).

[37]Heidegger, "Language in the Poem," in idem, *On the Way to Language,* trans. Peter D. Hertz (San Francisco: Harper & Row, 1971), 159–98.

peat the same suppressive gesture people accuse de Man of having committed.[38]

Derrida's reading is pertinent to my discussion of Heidegger's *Nietzsche*. No one who consciously experienced the time in which these texts arose will be able to read the dates of the lectures without thinking immediately of the military and political events surrounding them, which are consistently reflected in the writings. Apart from some turns in formulation, it cannot be claimed convincingly on the basis of these texts that Heidegger had separated himself from Nazism in 1935. The domination of the earth through racial breeding, the business-like organization of all beings, the simplification of all things and people into a controllable unity, and the program of total mechanization, among other features, still constitute in 1940 the ideal of the "grand style." To the extent, however, that the domination of the earth becomes untenable, the mood of these texts darkens to the grayest nihilism, a mood signaling the arrival of the "American epoch." It is in no way coincidental that the collapse of metaphysics in the history of Being occurs for Heidegger at the same time as the collapse of the Nazi Reich in the political world. The drama of Heidegger's epochal narrative is lost, however, if we do not also keep in mind his vision of this closing battle as the most vehement revolt of beings against Being, the inversion of Plato's heavenly ideas into mere drives here on earth.

[38]Jacques Derrida, "Like the Sound of the Sea Deep Within a Shell: Paul de Man's War," *Critical Inquiry* 14 (1988): 590–653.

◁□▷

2

Derrida

Although in his more recent works Derrida analyzes specific problems in Heidegger, considering, for example, only single terms (*Geist, Geschlecht,* and the hand), and at such moments becomes sharply critical, these later works share with the early writings a starting point in the critique of metaphysics and the criticism of philosophy.[1] Indeed, Derrida confronts Heidegger in each of his writings, and this confrontation is always, directly or indirectly, bound up with Nietzsche. Derrida has repeatedly emphasized the relationship of his thought to that of Heidegger and has consistently remarked that none of his investigations would have been possible "without the opening of Heidegger's questions" (*P,* 9). Above all, they "would not have been possible without the attention to what Heidegger calls the difference between Being and beings, the ontic-ontological difference such as, in a way, it remains unthought by philosophy" (*P,* 9). Despite this debt to Heidegger, "or rather because of it," Derrida continues to look for "the signs of a belonging to metaphysics" in Heidegger's texts, "or to what he calls onto-theology" (*P,* 10).

Such a procedure has in fact become a necessary and appro-

[1] Both German terms are notoriously difficult to translate, as they range in meaning from "mind" to "spirit" (*Geist*), and from "sex" to "race" or "lineage" (*Geschlecht*). See note 33 in Chapter 1 for references in Derrida's work, as well as *OS.*

priate task, because Heidegger's text is neither more "homogeneous" nor more "continuous" than any other text in philosophy and is not "everywhere equal to the greatest force and to all the consequences of its questions" (*P*, 10). Moreover, Heidegger recognized that "economically and strategically he had to borrow the syntactic and lexical resources of the language of metaphysics, as one always must do at the very moment that one deconstructs this language" (*P*, 10). Of primary concern to Derrida, then, in his confrontation with Heidegger is locating the attachments or "holds" of metaphysics ("prises de la métaphysique") on this philosophy. Of all these attachments, "the ultimate determination of difference as the ontic-ontological difference—however necessary and decisive this phase may be—still seems to me, in a strange way, to be in the grasp of metaphysics" (*P*, 10).

At this point, in a move characteristic of Derrida, Nietzsche enters the game. In order to think the truth of Being to its ultimate consequences and to think of this concept in a way that is not determined, as it is in the West, "as the difference between Being and beings" (*P*, 10), one should move "along lines that would be more Nietzschean than Heideggerian" (*P*, 10). Derrida immediately adds that such a step "is doubtless not possible today, but one could show how it is in preparation" (*P*, 10). Clearly, this Nietzsche is not the systematic figure constructed by Heidegger in his lectures but a Nietzsche with a previously unrecognized deconstructive ability.

A brief consideration of the essay "The Ends of Man" will show how Derrida's critique of Heidegger rapidly becomes an affirmation of Nietzsche's thought. This essay concerns the anthropological, humanistic, subject-oriented tendencies of contemporary philosophy, a kind of fundamentalism centered in "human reality" (*MP*, 109–36). In the *Letter on Humanism*, Heidegger had spoken out against just such a humanistic or subject-oriented philosophizing, particularly the kind that remains dominated by "the peculiar dictatorship of the public realm," the horizon of a self-certain and self-asserting humanity.[2] Derrida has, in opposition to humanistic interpreters of Heidegger like Sartre, shown "that anthropology and humanism were not the milieu of his thought and the horizon of his questions" (*MP*, 118) and turned in general against those who would banish "Hegel, Husserl, and Heidegger into the shadows of humanist metaphysics" (*MP*, 119).

In regard to the question, however, of how the *relève* or suspension "of man in the thought of Hegel, Husserl, and Heidegger" takes place (*MP*, 119), Derrida believes that "the thinking of the end of man" in the equivocal sense of an ending—namely as the "play of *telos* and death" (*MP*, 134)—"is always prescribed in metaphysics, in the thinking of the truth of man" (*MP*, 121). Thus for Heidegger, too, the question of the truth of Being is inseparable from the question of "the proper of man," those qualities that belong most characteristically to human beings (*MP*, 124). To be sure, the Dasein of Heideggerian philosophy is "not simply the man of metaphysics" (*MP*, 124). But in Heidegger there occurs "a more subtle, hidden, stubborn privilege" of the human, which with "the attraction of 'the proper of man' will not cease to direct all the itineraries of thought" (*MP*, 124). Once Heidegger asked the question of the meaning of Being in all its radicality, he had "to acknowledge the exemplary being which will constitute the privileged text for a reading of the meaning of Being" (*MP*, 125). This "being, which we are ourselves," does not have for Heidegger "the form of subjective consciousness, as in transcendental phenomenology," but involves "a continual bringing to light" (*MP*, 126). Upon closer analysis, however, it appears "that *Dasein*, though not man, is nevertheless *nothing other* than man" (*MP*, 127). It is, as Derrida remarks, "a repetition of the essence of man permitting a return to what is before the metaphysical concepts of *humanitas*" (*MP*, 127).

Heidegger suspends the authority of traditional metaphys-

[2]Martin Heidegger, *Letter on Humanism*, trans. Frank A. Capuzzi, in *BW*, 193–242, 197.

ics in order "to lead us to think the presence of the present"
(*MP*, 131). The "thinking of Being," the "thinking of the truth
of Being, in the name of which Heidegger delimits humanism
and metaphysics, remains a thinking *of* man." It is indeed "a
kind of reevaluation or revalorization of the essence and dignity of man," even an attempt to overcome the "threat to the
essence of humanity" that arises from the rapidly spreading
metaphysics of technology (*MP*, 128). The thought resists humanism "because it does not set the *humanitas* of man high
enough" (*MP*, 130). As Heidegger expressed it, this thinking
does not overcome metaphysics "by climbing still higher, sur-
mounting it, transcending it somehow or other; thinking over-
comes metaphysics by climbing back down into the nearness
of the nearest" (*MP*, 132). Bound up with such thought is a
"metaphorics of proximity, of simple and immediate presence," in which words like "neighboring, shelter, house, service, guard, voice, and listening" take precedence and inscribe
this language into "a certain landscape" (*MP*, 130).

Precisely at this point Nietzsche becomes significant for
Derrida, since it was Nietzsche who called our attention to
"this security of the near," "that is, the co-belonging and co-
propriety of the name of man and the name of Being" (*MP*,
133). At the same time it becomes evident that this critique or
deconstruction of Heidegger begins at a few levels deeper than
in the writings on Heidegger's usage of *Geist*, hand, and *Geschlecht*.[3] Here, the primary concern is the fundamental starting point of Heidegger's thought, the "condition of the possibility" of his philosophy, his "structural principle," namely,
the principle of the homeland, of proximity, of being, of presence, of identity. Nietzsche is, by contrast, the thinker who has
taught us to think difference, to speak several languages, and
to produce several texts simultaneously: "If there is style,
Nietzsche reminded us, it must be *plural*" (*MP*, 135).

This "suspension" or "relève" of human beings, announced

[3] See note 1 to this chapter.

by Nietzsche in the form of the *Übermensch*, occurs differently for him than it does for Heidegger, in such a way that the *Übermensch* "awakens and leaves, without turning back to what he leaves behind him":

> He burns his text and erases the traces of his steps. His laughter then will burst out, directed toward a return which no longer will have the form of the metaphysical repetition of humanism, nor, doubtless, "beyond" metaphysics, the form of a memorial or a guarding of the meaning of Being, the form of the house and of the truth of Being. He will dance, outside the house, the *aktive Vergesslichkeit*, the "active forgetting" and the cruel (*grausam*) feast of which the *Genealogy of Morals* speaks. (MP, 136)

Derrida adds: "No doubt that Nietzsche called for an active forgetting of Being: it would not have the metaphysical form imputed to it by Heidegger" (*MP*, 136). Nietzsche's active forgetting of Being is his conscious wish to free himself from the Being of Western metaphysics, whereas Heidegger's passive forgetting of Being leads only to the reconstruction of a new metaphysical framework such as the will to power.

The most prominent critique of Heidegger undertaken in Nietzsche's name appears at the beginning of *Grammatology*, published in 1967 (*G*, 3–26). Derrida's first large publication inevitably created the impression, because of its title, its size, and its academic manner of representation and organization, that he was taking a new step in the history of transcendental phenomenology as the philosopher of writing. In reality, the very image of the "unity of the book" (the "unity 'book' considered as a perfect totality"; *P*, 3) is questioned in this text, as indeed are all the accompanying manifestations ("the entirety of our culture"; *P*, 3) bound up with such an image. *Grammatology* is, in other words, just as much a *text* as Derrida's other writings; that is, it is a many-layered procedure "whose unfinished movement assigns itself no absolute beginning" (*P*, 3). Derrida has explained this procedure by suggesting that *Grammatology* consists of a long essay split into two parts, and that *Writing and Difference*, from the same year, could be inserted into the middle. Together these would form a collection of twelve essays, with the Rousseau text, which makes up the second part of *Grammatology*, as the "twelfth 'table'" of the collection (*P*, 4). On the other hand, as Derrida says, *Grammatology* could also be inserted into the middle of *Writing and Difference*, because many of these writings arose at the same time and some of the essays from this collection—for example, "Freud and the Scene of Writing" (*WD*, 196–231)—are obviously "engaged in the grammatological opening" (*P*, 4).

With these comments Derrida highlights the essayistic, non-systematic character of his writings. In the case of *Grammatology*, this seems especially appropriate, because many readers apparently have the impression, with good reason, that the text was meant to develop a systematic, positive science named "grammatology."[4] Indeed the first section reads for long passages as if it contains the design of a fundamental philosophy of writing, the many-layered text, and the multiply structured arrangement of signs. Derrida appeared to turn the semiological, structuralist principles of Saussure's "general course for a science of language" to the written text, and to derive a "general course for a science of writing." From this perspective the first part of *Grammatology* resembles the torso of an incomplete system that only seems to be followed by essays and fragments. Of course, the first part, with its "Preface," "Exergue," and "Program," could equally be read, perhaps with even more justification, as a parody of systematic writing that predictably reaches an impasse in its procedures and then crosses over into a more appropriately essayistic and fragmentary form of writing. For both of these readings, however, it is important that the decisive confrontation with Heidegger and Nietzsche takes place, in the section "The Written Being / The Being Written," under the semiological aspects of

[4]See Richard Rorty, "Philosophy as a Kind of Writing: An Essay on Derrida," in idem, *Consequences of Pragmatism* (Minneapolis: University of Minnesota Press, 1982), 90–109: "Thus [Derrida] warns us against taking 'grammatology' as the name of a new research program" (98).

writing and texts. It is useful to consider the formal, functional
mechanisms of the sign systems Derrida derives on the one
hand from the classical doctrines of the sign developed in
antiquity, the medieval period, and modern rationalism, and
on the other hand from twentieth-century linguistics and
structuralism.

As a distinctive component of his interpretation of Nietzsche, and in regard to his uses of both the classical and the
modern doctrines of the sign, Derrida's theory of writing
builds on the fundamental distinction between the voice
(*phonē*) and writing (*gramma*). For Derrida there occur in both
forms of semiology, with an inner necessity following from the
characteristic logic of Western thought, a privileging of the
voice as "the nonexterior, nonmundane, therefore nonempiri-
cal or noncontingent signifier" and, at the same time, a reduction of writing "to a secondary and instrumental function," to
the merely written "translator of a full speech that was fully
present" (*G*, 8). This relationship between the voice (spoken
word) and writing (the written text) is so pivotal to Derrida's
argument that it also shapes his image of Nietzsche, even at
those moments when the connections are not immediately visible. The conception of "'hearing (understanding)-oneself-
speak' through the phonic substance" informs, according to
Derrida, not only the entire Western "idea of the world," with
all its differentiations "between the worldly and the non-
worldly, the outside and the inside, ideality and nonideality,
universal and nonuniversal," but above all the "theme of presence" as "the basis of all metaphysics" (*G*, 7–8).

Admittedly the boundaries between the spoken and the
written sign cannot always be strictly maintained, insofar as in
a loose or metaphorical manner of expression speech will be
called writing or writing, speech. The priority of the spoken
word over the written in Western thought nowhere appears
more clearly than in the prominent conception of writing as
the mere reproduction of the spoken word, as "phonetic writing, the medium of the great metaphysical, scientific, technical,

and economic adventure of the West" (*G*, 10). Writing, from
this perspective essentially derivative, was brought about by
means of the spoken word together with the "instance of the
logos, or of a reason thought within the lineage of the logos, in
whatever sense it is understood: in the pre-Socratic or the
philosophical sense, in the sense of God's infinite understanding or in the anthropological sense, in the pre-Hegelian or the
post-Hegelian sense" (*G*, 10–11). In contrast to the muffled or
weakened writing of the classical or the modern tradition,
Derrida's theory can be characterized as the establishment of
an "enlarged and radicalized" writing (*G*, 10), a writing that
no longer issues from a logos and that, through the operations
of the voice and reason, is related to a meaning but now itself
has a decisive and originary character.

The derivative character of writing is seen in Plato in
the opposition between "bad writing (writing in the 'literal'
[*propre*] and ordinary sense, 'sensible' writing, 'in space')" and
"the writing of truth in the soul" (*G*, 15). For Aristotle, "spoken
words (*ta en tē phonē*) are the symbols of mental experience
(*pathēmata tēs psychēs*) and written words are the symbols of
spoken words" (*G*, 11). As the "producer of the first signifier,"
the voice "has a relationship of essential and immediate proximity with the mind" (*G*, 11). Each signifier is derivative, but
the voice is closer to the signified than is writing. Although in
modern semiology—for example for Saussure—signified and
signifier are "distinguished simply as the two faces of one and
the same leaf," in the classical doctrine of the sign there was
always implied "the distinction between signifier and signified" (*G*, 11), particularly in a strictly hierarchical sense. The
consequence Derrida draws from this hierarchical organization is characteristic for his position: "logocentrism" is also
"phonocentrism," "absolute proximity of voice and being, of
voice and the meaning of being, of voice and the ideality of
meaning" (*G*, 12). A further result of this traditional hierar-
chization is a familiar feature of Western metaphysics, the
"determination of the meaning of being in general as *pres-*

ence" with all its historical expressions, leading up to that self-reflexive act "by which, by virtue of hearing (understanding)-oneself-speak—an indissociable system—the subject affects itself and is related to itself in the element of ideality" (*G*, 12). The convergence of logocentrism with the "determination of the Being of beings as presence" is, for Derrida, one of the most important features of this complex. In order to relieve the abstraction in these deliberations and to move the discussion toward Nietzsche, the question could be raised—strictly as a kind of illustration—of whether Heidegger also clung to logocentrism and phonocentrism in his notion of presence, as well as to the hierarchical relation between the signified and the signifier. The answer would likely be that, on the one hand, Heidegger indeed remains captive in this "epoch of onto-theology, within the philosophy of presence," that closure which had already shown itself but outside of which he was unable to step (*G*, 12). On the other hand, Heidegger more than anyone has announced the end of this epoch. Derrida gives this reply to the question of Heidegger's position in history: "The movements of belonging or not belonging to the epoch are too subtle, the illusions in that regard are too easy, for us to make a definite judgment" (*G*, 12). Evidently such an equivocal conclusion could be drawn not only for Heidegger but also for Nietzsche and Derrida as well.

In "the epoch of the logos," at any rate, writing is "debased," considered the "mediation of mediation and as a fall into the exteriority of meaning" (*G*, 12–13). Writing is degraded into the merely visible aspect of the sign, exiled "into the exteriority of the sensible here below," whereas the voice, as the "intelligible face of the sign," "remains turned toward the word and the face of God" (*G*, 13). This "epoch of the logos" is therefore essentially "theological": "The sign and divinity have the same place and time of birth" (*G*, 14). Derrida refers here not only to the medieval concept of the sign, from the era of Aquinas and Dante, but also to every sign theory that attempts "to withdraw meaning, truth, presence, being, etc., from the movement of signification" (*G*, 14) and tries to establish itself beyond writing and interpretation. This classical tradition of the sign has been under siege "for about a century," as Derrida remarks; the mistrust of the sign apparent in recent theory does not relate to a truth "superior to the sign," but on the contrary relies on a concept of the sign that is just as historically and necessarily part of metaphysics (*G*, 14).

How is this to be understood? In 1873, nearly a century before the publication of *Grammatology* in 1967, Nietzsche wrote "On Truth and Lie in an Extra-Moral Sense," a text that formulates exactly that mistrust of classical semiotics to which Derrida is referring.[5] Central to this theory of writing are the "exteriority of the signifier" and "exteriority of writing in general." "Within this epoch reading and writing, the production or interpretation of signs, the text in general as fabric of sign, allow themselves to be confined within secondariness" (*G*, 14). They are secondary in opposition to a truth and a meaning "already constituted by and within the element of the logos" (*G*, 14).

For Derrida, however, it is important to see that "there is no linguistic sign before writing," so that *eo ipso* in classical times "the very idea of the sign falls into decay" (*G*, 14). This theory, predictably enough, has caused much confusion and produced many misunderstandings, since it appears to insinuate a reversal of the classical and traditional understandings of the relationship of the voice to writing. Whereas in the classical tradition the spoken sign enjoyed priority over the written sign, now writing seems to be prioritized over speech—an obviously absurd claim that would quickly be disputed by any child psychologist or cultural anthropologist. Derrida, however, is concerned not with a reversal of priorities but rather with a theory of writing that pays sufficient attention to the scriptibil-

[5] The most recent translation is entitled "On Truth and Lying in an Extra-Moral Sense," in *Friedrich Nietzsche on Rhetoric and Language*, trans. and ed. Sander L. Gilman, Carole Blair, and David J. Parent (New York: Oxford University Press, 1989), 246–57.

ity or textuality of language and that tries to deconstruct the hierarchy of voice over writing. His aim is to analyze their interweavings and reciprocities more precisely. What we ordinarily call "writing in the literal sense" is "a writing that is sensible, finite" (*G*, 15). This kind of writing is most often "thought on the side of culture, technique, and artifice," and we see in it "a human procedure, the ruse of a being accidentally incarnated or of a finite creature" (*G*, 15). To stress the finite character of writing, we relegate it to a derivative, inferior position as mere metaphor and dismiss it as a reflection of something prior, higher, nobler, in brief, a metaphor. This contradictory devaluation occurs not only in the relationships of writing to voice, meaning, truth, and the logos but also in the numerous metaphorical comparisons of finite, ordinary, human writing with a more perfect writing like that of God, the Book of Nature, the earth, and the world, which our writing is unable to grasp. Derrida cites numerous examples from this literature, including the statements of a certain Rabbi Eliezer.[6] These not only are among the most impressive of his citations, but have led to an acutely ironic misunderstanding in recent literature.[7] The citation begins: "If all the seas were of ink, and all ponds planted with reeds, if the sky and the earth were parchments and if all human beings practiced the art of writing—they would not exhaust the Torah I have learned" (*G*, 16). Of course, such passages do not amount to a glorification of these infinite writings. They show, rather, how the "system of signified truth" and a predetermined meaning have always already been used to discredit "human and laborious, finite and artificial, inscription" (*G*, 15). In other words these illustrations explore the inscribed quality of script, the

[6]Cf. Emmanuel Levinas, in *Difficile liberté: Essais sur le judaisme* (Paris: Albin Michel, 1963), 44 (*G*, 324). For Derrida's interpretation of Levinas's work, see "Violence and Metaphysics: An Essay on the Thought of Emmanuel Levinas" (*WD*, 79–153).

[7]Habermas, for example, characterizes Derrida as a "Jewish mystic" who wants to drain the pond with black ink (*DM*, 182).

textual character of texts, and the metaphoricity of writing (*G*, 16).

A further refinement in the theory of "fallen writing" appeared in the seventeenth and eighteenth centuries, along with the subjectivism of a self-sublimating rationality: "It is non-self-presence that will be denounced" (*G*, 17). This discourse, of central importance for Derrida, is more fully discussed in the second part of *Grammatology* because it is represented most strongly by Rousseau: "Rousseau repeats the Platonic gesture by referring to another model of presence: self-presence in the senses, in the sensible cogito, which simultaneously carries in itself the inscription of divine law" (*G*, 17). In opposition to this self-presence in the senses, Rousseau condemns writing and describes it as a corpse. On the other hand, however, there is also good and bad writing for Rousseau: "The good and natural is the divine inscription in the heart and the soul; the perverse and artful is technique, exiled in the exteriority of the body" (*G*, 17).

The primary contrast for Derrida, however, is between writing and the work, or better, the book, as a self-enclosed "totality, finite or infinite, of the signifier" (*G*, 18). Book and work rest on the presupposition that "a totality constituted by the signified"—such as truth or meaning—exists prior to inscription, which "supervises its inscriptions and its signs, and is independent of it in its ideality" (*G*, 18). We operate according to such a presupposition when, in our own readings, we attribute a definitive meaning to a text. This move reasserts a singular truth and thus projects an image of the text as a book or a work. Derrida explains: "The idea of the book, which always refers to a natural totality, is profoundly alien to the sense of writing. It is the encyclopedic protection of theology and of logocentrism against the disruption of writing, against its aphoristic energy, and, as I shall specify later, against difference in general" (*G*, 18).

The distinguishing of the text from the book "denudes the surface of the text" (*G*, 18). It is also clear that the reduction of writing or the text to the book or the work has nowhere taken place more radically than in the case of Nietzsche. His editors compiled, from the mass of his notebooks, what Elisabeth Förster-Nietzsche called his "philosophical prose masterpiece." Heidegger, deliberately ignoring of the texts written by Nietzsche himself, chose the resulting book, *The Will to Power*, as the primary object of interpretation. On this basis he was able to think together the two thoughts of the will to power and the eternal recurrence of the same, which had previously seemed incomplete and unevenly articulated, as Nietzsche's "actual" thought pertaining to Western metaphysics and the truth of the Being of beings, and to highlight this thought in its "correct" proportions.

With this reading of Nietzsche, the classical treatment of the sign, or the classical procedure of hermeneutics, reached its culmination. At the same time the radicalization of "the concepts of *interpretation, perspective, evaluation, difference*" (*G*, 19), which Nietzsche had accomplished in his texts, was diminished. Instead of remaining simply "within metaphysics," as Heidegger wished, Nietzsche contributed substantially to "the liberation of the signifier from its dependence or derivation with respect to the logos and the related concept of truth or the primary signified, in whatever sense that is understood" (*G*, 19). Reading, writing, and the text were for Nietzsche "'originary' operations" (*G*, 19). He did not transcribe a meaning and inscribe a truth in the "presence of the logos, as *topos noētos*, divine understanding, or the structure of a priori necessity" (*G*, 19). As Derrida sees it, "The virulence of Nietzschean thought could not be more completely misunderstood" (*G*, 19).

But perhaps, Derrida suggests in this 1967 text, when faced with such a procedure we should not "protect Nietzsche from the Heideggerian reading, we should perhaps offer him up to it completely, underwriting that interpretation without reserve" (*G*, 19). Derrida argues that Heidegger should be seconded "in a *certain way*," to the point at which the form of Nietzsche's discourse "regains its absolute strangeness" for this interpretation, "where his text finally invokes a different type of reading, more faithful to his type of writing" (*G*, 19). At this point Derrida turns against Heidegger's recasting of Nietzsche's writing as a book. Derrida says: "Nietzsche has *written what* he has written. He has written that writing—and first of all his own—is not originarily subordinate to the logos and to truth. And that this subordination has *come into being* during an epoch whose meaning we must deconstruct" (*G*, 19). According to Heidegger's reading, "the Nietzschean demolition remains dogmatic and, like all reversals, a captive of that metaphysical edifice which it professes to overthrow" (*G*, 19). In the "*order of reading*," the conclusions of Heidegger, like those of Eugen Fink, are in fact "irrefutable" (*G*, 20).[8] However, Heidegger's thought, which underlies this reading, does not at all destroy "the instance of the logos and of the truth of being as *primum signatum*," but reinstates it. This primum signatum, this "first signified" in the transcendental sense, is implied by "all categories or all determined significations, by all lexicons and all syntax, and therefore by all linguistic signifiers," and remains "irreducible to all the epochal determinations" (*G*, 20). With this the "history of the logos" is opened. According to this history everything exists inside the logos; outside of the logos nothing exists (*G*, 20). The primum signatum, the logos of being, is thus "the first and the last resource of the sign, of the difference between *signans* and *signatum*" (*G*, 20).

In the further elaboration of this thought, Derrida states that experience for Heidegger manifests itself as the "experience of 'being'" (*G*, 20), so that the word *being*, whether as an "originary word" (*Urwort*) or as the "transcendental word," assures "the possibility of being-word to all other words" and thus is "precomprehended in all language" (*G*, 20). This touches on the problematic opening of *Being and Time*, in

[8]Eugen Fink, *La philosophie de Nietzsche* (Paris: Minuit, 1965). The French translation was far more influential than the German original (*Nietzsches Philosophie*, Stuttgart: Kohlhammer, 1960), which went almost unnoticed.

which Heidegger raises anew "the question of the meaning of Being" as the necessary and prior question for all thinking.[9] Of greater importance here is the question of how Heidegger accomplishes the "breakthrough" out of this circle of metaphysics. He does this, according to Derrida, through "the *question* of being" that he asks metaphysics: "And with it the question of truth, of sense, of the logos" (*G*, 22). This questioning "does not restore confidence"; instead, it examines "the state just before all determinations of being, destroying the securities of onto-theology," and contributes, "quite as much as contemporary linguistics, to the dislocation of the unity of the sense of being, that is, in the last instance, the unity of the word" (*G*, 22).

Heidegger's questioning of Being also provides a metaphor for "the ambiguity of the Heideggerian situation with respect to the metaphysics of presence and logocentrism" (*G*, 22). The "voice of Being" becomes here "silent, mute, insonorous, wordless" (*G*, 22). Between the "voice of Being" (the original meaning of Being) and the "call of Being" (articulated sound), there arises a "rupture" (*G*, 22). Heidegger here remains "contained" within the metaphysics of presence and "transgresses" it: "The very movement of transgression sometimes holds it back short of the limit" (*G*, 22). In addition, the "meaning of Being" for Heidegger is "never simply and rigorously a 'signified'" (*G*, 22). On the other hand, it is also "literally neither 'primary,' nor 'fundamental,' nor 'transcendental,' whether understood in the scholastic, Kantian, or Husserlian sense" (*G*, 22). Heidegger further recalls that even the privileged "Being," in its "general syntactic and lexicological forms," remains rooted "in a system of languages and an historically determined 'significance,'" although he calls on us "to meditate on the 'privilege' of the 'third person singular of the present indicative' and the 'infinitive'" (*G*, 23).

Through these various operations, Heidegger maintains "a

[9]*BAT*, 1.

questioning of what constitutes our history and what produced transcendentality itself" (*G*, 23). This occurs in a particularly impressive fashion in his study *The Question of Being*. [10] Heidegger lets the word *Being* be read "only if it is crossed out (*kreuzweise Durchstreichung*)" (*G*, 23). The gesture, Derrida adds, is not a "merely negative symbol": "That deletion is the final writing of an epoch. Under its strokes the presence of a transcendental signified is effaced while still remaining legible. Is effaced while still remaining legible, is destroyed while making visible the very idea of the sign. Inasmuch as it de-limits onto-theology, the metaphysics of presence and logocentrism, this last writing is also the first writing" (*G*, 23).

Since, however, the "breakthrough" and the "transgression" engineered by Heidegger are not yet prepared by any type of discourse, these movements may themselves become "regressive": instead of moving "at and beyond onto-theology," they may return to the concepts of a primordial homeland or absolute proximity (*G*, 23). For Derrida, by contrast, we face the task of pushing further, into the realm of "différance," which "by itself would be more 'originary'" than the ontic-ontological difference posited by Heidegger, although "one would no longer be able to call it 'origin' or 'ground'" (*G*, 23). [11] We are concerned here with the "more Nietzschean than Heideggerian step" mentioned earlier, which would lead to a différance "that is no longer determined, in the language of the West, as the difference between Being and beings" (*P*, 10). This Nietzschean step toward différance can best be followed, however, from the perspective of the new linguistics and structural semiology.

The "logocentric" and "ethnocentric" models, which for Derrida also determine the concept of the sign used in modern semiology, are more closely described in a dialogue between Derrida and Julia Kristeva. His statements there outline the

[10] *QB*, see esp. 80–84.
[11] The distinctive spelling of the word will be clarified below.

derivation of his own notion of writing and offer the clearest explanation of his conception of "différance." These thoughts lead more directly into the nature of the différance of writing and text and reveal much more of Derrida's sense of Nietzsche's text than do the reflections arising from his consideration of the hierarchical *signans-signatum* relationship of the classical doctrine of signs. For even if, as Derrida says, the modern concept of the sign, "by its roots and its implications, is in all its aspects metaphysical . . . in systematic solidarity with stoic and medieval theology," it has nevertheless produced displacements in the theory of the sign that "have had delimiting effects" (*P*, 17). In any case the modern theory of the sign has made possible the "simultaneous *marking* and *loosening* of the limits of the system in which this concept was born and began to serve" (*P*, 17).

Derrida takes as his primary example of modern sign theory the "semiology of the Saussurean type," both as it emerged at the beginning of the twentieth century with the publication in 1916 of Ferdinand de Saussure's *Course in General Linguistics* and as it found its most important expression in French structuralism (*P*, 18). Against the traditional theory of the sign, this semiology exercised "an absolutely decisive critical role": it showed "that the signified is inseparable from the signifier, that the signified and signifier are the two sides of one and the same production," or, in Saussure's formulation, that "a two-sided unity" is established (*P*, 18). Moreover, and in a sense directly relevant to Derrida's concept of differential writing, Saussure emphasized "the differential and formal characteristics of semiological functioning" (*P*, 18).

At this point Derrida refers to Saussure's renovations of the concept of language. Language is, from this perspective, a system of signs in which the relation of the signs to what they signify (words to things, linguistic expressions to ideas) is not natural, "ontic," or inevitable in any sense, but "arbitrary." Of course, there are onomatopoetic constructions ("sub aqua" = "frog"; Ovid) and other word combinations ("type-writer") that seem exceptions to this rule. But basically the designations "Baum," "tree," or "arbre" do not spring out of the ground of Being. They are arbitrary within the given system of language and have meaning only within this system. The signs of language are not autonomous instances in themselves but elements of a system. They are determined positively not by what they are but negatively, by what they are not, by their differences from the other elements of the system. They are what the others are not. Language, in this respect, is not a system of identities. It is a system of differences.

According to Derrida, however, the momentous possibilities implied by the new conception were overlooked, perhaps unavoidably, and the model fell back into metaphysics. This occurred primarily because Saussure, lacking any other concept for the relation he saw between the signifier and the signified ("a two-sided unity"), reintroduced the concept of the sign and necessarily assumed "at least some of the implications inscribed in its system" (*P*, 19). The concept of the sign assumes what Derrida calls the "transcendental signified," an endpoint in the series of significations "which in and of itself, in its essence, would refer to no signifier, would exceed the chain of signs, and would no longer itself function as a signifier" (*P*, 19–20). For Derrida such an assumption is suspect, since each signified entity also plays the role of a signifier.[12] Saussure's return to a "transcendental signified" and the attempt to ground his thought in it is, according to Derrida, "not being imposed from without by something like 'philosophy'" but results automatically from "everything that links our language, our culture, our 'system of thought' to the history and system of metaphysics" (*P*, 20).

Saussure's regressions can be seen, for example, in his privileging of the "phonic substance" of the voice (*P*, 21), when he viewed linguistics as "the regulatory model, the 'pattern,' for a

---

[12]"The signified is ... *always already in the position of the signifier*" (*G*, 73).

general semiology of which it was to be, by all rights and theoretically, only a part" (*P*, 21). In any case the "theme of the
arbitrary," the principle of arbitrariness that marked the new
linguistics, was "turned away from its most fruitful paths (for-
malization) toward a hierarchizing teleology" (*P*, 21). The focus should have been the ability to create a "system of distinct
signs," "the possibility of the code and of articulation, independent of any substance, for example, phonic substance," and not
the production of a spoken language (*P*, 21).

Similarly, Derrida saw in the modern concept of structure a
phenomenon that could "simultaneously confirm and shake
logocentric and ethnocentric assuredness" (*P*, 24). As with the
concept of signs, the concept of structure is "as old as the 'episteme'—that is to say, as old as Western science and Western
philosophy" (*WD*, 278). In the older phases of the tradition, we
find the concept of structure designated as "unity," "order,"
"connection," or "system." The ability to think the "structurality of structure" (*WD*, 278) was always one of the strengths
of philosophy and had been part of it from its inception. The
essential concept of the "structurality of structure," however,
"although it has always been at work," has "always been neutralized or reduced" by the process of "giving it a center or of
referring it to a point of presence, a fixed origin" (*WD*, 278).

Yet given such a center and origin, or such a presence, something was imagined that lay outside the structure and could
not be unified with the concept of the pure structurality of
structure. As Derrida describes it, "The function of this center
was not only to orient, balance, and organize the structure—
one cannot in fact conceive of an unorganized structure—but
above all to make sure that the organizing principle of the
structure would limit what we might call the *play* of the structure" (*WD*, 278). The "play of the elements" thus seemed
bound "inside the total form" (*WD*, 279). This bonded image
engraved itself so strongly into Western philosophical consciousness that "the notion of a structure lacking any center
represents the unthinkable itself" (*WD*, 279).

The center that sets a limit to the play of the elements is something that both escapes the structurality of structure and controls it. It could therefore be said that this center lies outside the structure; but since it controls the structure, it simultaneously has an impact inside. In this "contradictory way" the "concept of the centered structure" is coherent: it is "the concept of a play based on a fundamental ground, a play constituted on the basis of a fundamental immobility and a reassuring certitude, which itself is beyond the reach of play" (*WD*, 279). This contradictory concept of coherence, which "represents coherence itself, the condition of the episteme as philosophy or science," "expresses the force of a desire" for Derrida (*WD*, 279). Through the "certainty" that imagines itself removed from play, "anxiety can be mastered, for anxiety is invariably the result of a certain mode of being implicated in the game, of being caught by the game, of being as it were at stake in the game from the outset" (*WD*, 279).

This is Derrida's argument about the classical concept of structure, a system in which all events—"repetitions, substitutions, transformations, and permutations"—are "implicated" in a "history of meaning," a history in which full "presence" receives the name of the "origin or the end, of *archē* or of *telos*" (*WD*, 279). The history of Western philosophy, at least in its classical period or until Hegel, appears from this perspective "as a series of substitutions of center for center" that certify, limit, and control the structurality of structure. These centers have received a series of different names: "The history of metaphysics, like the history of the West, is the history of these metaphors and metonymies" (*WD*, 279). Their "matrix" would be "the determination of Being as *presence* in all senses of this word" (*WD*, 279). From Heidegger's history of Being, we know the main stations in this sequence: idea, God, transcendental cogito, transcendental apperception, will to power. Derrida makes finer distinctions in his list, although this history of Being is not particularly crucial for him, nor does it distract him from the thought of the structurality of structure.

At the outset it was suggested that with the writings of Nietzsche, Freud, and Heidegger, a "break" or "rupture" had occurred in the classical concept of structure. Now the center or the "transcendental signified" of structure is no longer thought of as a stable presence outside structure but as a function inside structure itself, as a sign among signs. With this realization it appeared "that there was no center, that the center could not be thought in the form of a present-being, that the center had no natural site, that it was not a fixed locus but a function, a sort of nonlocus in which an infinite number of sign-substitutions came into play" (*WD*, 280). With this "absence of a center or origin," everything changed from the ground up, everything now became "discourse," and "the domain and the play of signification" were extended "infinitely" (*WD*, 280). Derrida sees the same breakthrough to the thought of the pure structurality of structure in the formal context of semiology, with Saussure's new linguistics and with the structural ethnology of Lévi-Strauss. But just as Saussure lost the pure thought of structure by privileging voice, Lévi-Strauss gave preference to archaic or natural social forms over the artificial ones of culture and therefore remained equally bound to a kind of thinking that wanted to move back more closely and precisely to the origins of the true and the genuine (*WD*, 281–93).

Derrida argued in conversation with Kristeva that Saussure, like Plato, Aristotle, Rousseau, Hegel, and Husserl, among others, excluded writing "as a phenomenon of exterior representation, both useless and dangerous" (*P*, 25). For Saussure this must have appeared fully justified, since he had only the model of "phonetic-alphabetic" script in mind, which gives the impression of presenting speech "and at the same time" of erasing "itself before speech" (*P*, 25). In contrast, Derrida tries to show that "there is no purely phonetic writing, and that phonologism is less a consequence of the practice of the alphabet in a given culture than a certain ethical or axiological experience of this practice" (*P*, 25). If this experience were to be determined more precisely, then it could be said: "Writing should erase itself before the plenitude of living speech, perfectly represented in the transparency of its notation, immediately present for the subject who speaks it, and for the subject who receives its meaning, content, value" (*P*, 25).

The most important point for Derrida, however, is "not only not to privilege one substance—here the phonic, so-called temporal, substance—while excluding another—for example, the graphic, so called spatial, substance—but even to consider every process of signification as a formal play of differences" (*P*, 26). Only then can "the formal play of differences" be maintained (*P*, 26). The question may arise as to how we can begin the project of grammatology, and with it the very concepts of writing and of text, "when we seem to have neutralized every substance, be it phonic, graphic, or otherwise?" (*P*, 26) The answer is that we cannot return to the classical concept of writing as the imitation of the voice, nor can we simply invert "the dissymmetry that now has become problematical" (*P*, 26). It is a question rather of constructing a much broader and more radical concept of writing, which in its specific sense is called "gramma" but in its more general sense is called "différance," and which comprises every kind of articulation, communication, and coding (phonic, graphic, artistic). The primary characteristic of this writing is the "play of differences." During this play there are indeed syntheses and references, but never such that a "simple element" would be "present in and of itself, referring only to itself" (*P*, 26).

The text is such a chain of signs, in which there are "only, everywhere, differences and traces of traces" (*P*, 26). Stated semiologically, the gramma would be the most general sign, and semiology would be reconstituted as grammatology (*P*, 26). Since the gramma "is a structure and a movement no longer conceivable on the basis of the opposition presence / absence" but exists fully in the "play of differences," it would be better to call the new semiology "différance" instead of "grammatology." On the basis of its function alone, différance is inherently incompatible "with the static, synchronic, taxonomic, ahistoric motifs in the concept of structure" (*P*, 27). On the other hand, it is not "astructural" (*P*, 28). The "systematic and regulated transformations" in it are able at certain points but not at others to make room for a "structural science" (*P*, 28). One can even say that différance "develops the most legitimate principled exigencies of 'structuralism'" (*P*, 28). It cannot be said, however, that some kind of "present and in-different being" ("aucun étant présent et in-différant") precedes or changes into différance, for example, a subject "who would be the agent, author, and master of différance," or on whom différance would thrust itself (*P*, 28). Subjectivity is instead "an effect of différance, an effect inscribed within the system of différance" (*P*, 28).

The most concise text for clarifying these complexities is the famous lecture "La Différance," which Derrida delivered to the Société française de la philosophie on January 27, 1968, and which has since appeared in numerous editions.[13] The French verb *différer*, like the Latin *differre*, has two different meanings, "to differentiate" and "to delay," and hence expresses difference in two fundamentally different ways: "On the one hand, it indicates difference as distinction, inequality, or discernibility; on the other, it expresses the interposition of delay, the interval of a spacing and temporalizing that puts off until 'later' what is presently denied, the possible that is presently impossible" (*SP*, 129). With his use of the letter "a" from the present participle "différante," Derrida constructs a noun with a visibly written, however inaudible, spelling change, "différance" (as opposed to the usual spelling "différence"), which is meant to express both meanings of differentiation: as spatiotemporality and as the movement that structures every kind of dissociation, difference as deferral and as different (*SP*,

---

[13]Jacques Derrida, "La Différance," in idem, *Marges de la philosophie* (Paris: Minuit, 1972), 1–30. English translations include idem, "Différance," in *SP*, 129–60; and idem, "Différance," in *MP*, 1–27.

129–30). The "a" in the monstrous word "différance" is thus no printing error but an intentional addition by Derrida, in order to make difference even more different from itself than it already usually is.

However, since différance now not only is to be seen as the characteristic of script and an attribute of writing but begins to acquire the dimensions of a philosophical principle, Derrida seems to have returned irrevocably to the practices of that very philosophy of origin he has criticized, practices that would lead to a metaphysics of presence and identity and would characterize these as différance. But this assumption distorts the intended sense of différance; différance is in no way meant to suggest an alternative to presence or an overturning of the traditional system, since that would achieve a mere reversal of the system and would not disperse metaphysics. The task is not to represent différance as the opponent but as the inhabitant of that identity, not to detach it from structure through atomization but through function, and not to reveal différance as a suspension or sublimation but as the mode of subsistence for meaning and truth.

In his text, Derrida repeatedly suggests that différance appears best suited to think the "irreducibility" of our "epoch": "the juncture—rather than the summation—of what has been most decisively inscribed in the thought of what is conveniently called our 'epoch'" (*SP*, 130). He indicates that our "epoch" can be summarized as "the de-limitation of ontology (of presence)" (*SP*, 153). As examples of thinking in terms of différance, he adduces, in addition to Saussure's principle of semiological difference, the differentiation of force in Nietzsche, the possibility of "facilitation" and the delayed effect ("delay") in Freud, the irreducibility of the trace of the other in Emmanuel Levinas, and the ontic-ontological difference in Heidegger. These names and themes should indicate that the transgression of Western metaphysics through the concept of différance not only is at work in the linguistics and semiotics of structuralism but has also begun to be active in recent historical, philosophical, and psychoanalytical discourses.

The essay pursues the impossible task suggested here, a task perhaps best described as a preliminary move into a zone that our language blocks from articulation. Nearly all words and concepts related to the characterization of difference, particularly terms like interval, division, retention, and protention, rest on the metaphysics of presence and identity that is to be decentered. This linguistic indisposition, if it can be described with such a negative term, is for Derrida, however, only another manifestation of différance. Language is not the effect of a speaking subject; rather, the subject is inscribed in language and is itself a part of the play of différance.

Seen from this perspective, différance is "neither a *word* nor a *concept*" (*SP*, 130). It cannot be "exposed," since one can expose only "what, at a certain moment, can become present, manifest; what can be shown, presented as a present, a being-present in its truth, the truth of a present or the presence of a present" (*SP*, 134). Différance has neither existence nor essence and cannot even be defined in the sense of negative theology. Indeed, différance is not only "irreducible to every ontological or theological—onto-theological—reappropriation, but it opens up the very space in which onto-theology—philosophy—produces its system and its history. It thus encompasses and irrevocably surpasses onto-theology or philosophy" (*SP*, 135). With its alogical structure, différance also prohibits a linear structuring of the reading, for example, the ordering of reasons, any strategy of a final purpose, tactics of the telos, "philosophical-logical discourse," and its symmetrical opposite, "logico-empirical speech" (*SP*, 135). What remains for discussion beyond these traditional alternatives of philosophical discourse is the efficacy of play, and one way of pursuing the potentialities of différance consists in the semiotic dimensions of play.

These positions, bound up with the elimination of the "authority of presence" of the first or transcendental signified, should be clear from the previous argument. Another way of elaborating différance follows from the pioneers in this area—Nietzsche, Freud, Saussure, Heidegger, and Levinas. Nietzsche and Freud are particularly useful examples in this context, because they both, "as we know, and often in a very similar way, questioned the self-assured certitude of consciousness" (*SP*, 148). The crucial point for Derrida is "that both of them did this by starting out with the theme of différance" (*SP*, 148).

With Nietzsche the awareness of différance appears in his argument that "the important main activity is unconscious," that "consciousness is the effect of forces whose essence, ways, and modalities are not peculiar to it" (*SP*, 148). Nevertheless, the force determining consciousness is itself never present: "it is only a play of differences and quantities" (*SP*, 148). In Derrida's interpretation, the principle of différance in Nietzsche corresponds exactly to a "symptomatology" that diagnoses "the evasions and ruses of anything disguised in its différance" (*SP*, 149). Nietzsche's interpretation in general, however, is not "the disclosure of truth as a presentation of the thing itself in its presence, etc." but "an incessant deciphering" (*SP*, 149). For this kind of never-ending deciphering, Derrida uses the concept of "active interpretation." It rests on a "cipher without truth" or "a system of ciphers that is not dominated by truth value" (*SP*, 149). Truth value becomes "a function that is understood, inscribed, and circumscribed" (*SP*, 149). And Nietzsche, according to Derrida, posited "this 'active' (in movement) discord of the different forces and of the differences between forces" in opposition to the "system of metaphysical grammar, wherever that system controls culture, philosophy, and science" (*SP*, 149).

With Freud, the questioning of the domination of presence as consciousness turned to a questioning of the authority of consciousness. The two meanings of différance as differentiation and deferral are linked in Freud's theory, particularly in the concepts of the trace, facilitation, memory, inscription, and deferral itself. Derrida emphasizes the concept of deferral in Freud's *Beyond the Pleasure Principle*, which suggests that the self's drive toward self-preservation motivates a temporary replacement of the pleasure principle by the reality principle, but without "giving up the intention of an ultimate increase in pleasure," and thus "requires temporary patience towards displeasure on the long path towards pleasure."[14]

Nietzsche occupies an even more prominent position in "La Différance" as the chief proponent of the concept of différance. Characteristically, the reference occurs in conjunction with Heidegger, for Heidegger is for Derrida among the innovators of the new concept, and indeed the entire conclusion of the essay is devoted to him. Here it is no longer necessary, however, to mention all Derrida's doubts as to whether the ontic-ontological difference is "still an intrametaphysical effect of différance" or already the full "deployment of différance" (*SP*, 153). On the one hand, it can be said that "in a particular and very strange way, différance [is] 'older' than the ontological difference or the truth of Being" (*SP*, 154). On the other hand, however, no one knew better the "epochality" of his own history of Being than Heidegger. Derrida himself insists that we "must stay within the difficulty of this passage; we must repeat this passage in a rigorous reading of metaphysics, wherever metaphysics serves as the norm of Western speech, and not only in the texts of 'the history of philosophy'" (*SP*, 154).

These techniques of double gesticulation are now familiar. Derrida poses a more fundamental question when he asks of Being posited by Heidegger outside the chain of signification: "How do we conceive of the outside of a text?" (*SP*, 158) The question not only is related to the epochality of Western metaphysics and the problem of how texts apart from Western metaphysics relate but also concerns the more fundamental problem of whether we can move beyond the history of Being in general or move into "another language, outside the finite system of our language" (*SP*, 159). This was always the motivating aim of metaphysics as revealed in the attempts to name

[14]Sigmund Freud, *Beyond the Pleasure Principle*, in idem, *The Standard Edition of the Complete Psychological Works of Sigmund Freud*, vol. 18, ed. James Strachey (London, 1959).

the Being of beings, to center the structurality of structure, and to transcend play through the authority of a *primum signatum*. Heidegger was the most eloquent critic of these attempts. Yet he, too, conceived of an "outside of the text," an "exterior to the text," when he spoke with nostalgia for the truth of the Being of beings or preserved hope for a "marriage between speech and Being in the unique word, in the finally proper name" (*SP*, 160).

For Derrida there is no such transcendental realm: "There is nothing outside of the text" (or: "There is no outside-text: *il n'y a pas de hors-texte*"; *G*, 158), or "There will be no unique name, not even the name of Being" (*SP*, 159). But this must be thought without "nostalgia," "outside the myth of the purely maternal or paternal language belonging to the lost fatherland of thought" (*SP*, 159). "On the contrary," Derrida writes, "we must *affirm* it—in the sense that Nietzsche brings affirmation into play—with a certain laughter and with a certain dance" (*SP*, 159). In another passage Derrida distinguishes between "the Nietzschean *affirmation*" as a joyous affirmation of play and the "saddened, negative, nostalgic, guilty, Rousseauistic side of the thinking of play" (*WD*, 292). Nietzsche's "affirmation of the play of the world and of the innocence of becoming" is the "affirmation of a world of signs without fault, without truth, and without origin" (*WD*, 292), which stands open to our active interpretation. This active, affirmative interpretation consists, again, in recognizing "*the noncenter otherwise than as loss of the center*" and entering into play "without security" (*WD*, 292).

◁□▷

3

Nietzsche

In contrast to Heidegger's *Nietzsche*, Derrida's few statements about Nietzsche to date suggest an entirely antithetical image of that philosopher. A brief catalogue can be made of the primary traits of Derrida's Nietzsche. First, Nietzsche is distinctive for a decidedly anti-conventional concept of the sign, namely, that of a "sign without present truth" (*WD*, 280). The Nietzschean sign dispenses with every type of present truth, especially the notion of a truth with a fixed or finally determinate meaning, and thus it encourages a new type of interpretation. This interpretation is no longer satisfied by the appeal to a transcendental signified or to any other legitimizing ground but operates as an "incessant deciphering," the infinite practice of interpretation (*MP*, 18; *G*, 19). Interpretation as carried out by Nietzsche can also be described as the joyous affirmation of the world as play (*WD*, 292). "Nietzsche reminded us," Derrida argues, that the style or writing appropriate to such thought "must be *plural*" (*MP*, 135).

Derrida has delineated several other features of Nietzsche: for example, the distinctive "symptomatology" that operates with cunning and dissimulation and frequently guides its diagnoses toward the opposite of what is expected or most obvious. These features are connected to the several themes mentioned above, since Nietzsche's symptomatology relates directly to his concept of signs. The primary features of Derrida's Nietzsche involve the themes of the *sign, interpretation, play*, and *style*.

This image of Nietzsche, however, so radically contradicts not only the Nietzsche interpretation developed by Heidegger but also nearly all the traditional interpretations of Nietzsche, with the possible exception of Jaspers's (see Chapter 1), that the question arises of the relation between the image and Nietzsche's own text.

Even Jaspers's *Nietzsche*, with its clear awareness of infinite interpretation, the game of the world, and the multiple style of communication, almost entirely ignores the semiological aspect emphasized by Derrida. To be sure, the linguistic aspects of Nietzsche's text and the themes pertinent to the philosophy of language had been noticed early in the research on Nietzsche.[1] In an article published in 1890, for example, Fritz Mauthner saw the philosophy of language as Nietzsche's essential focus.[2] Some of Nietzsche's assertions, such as "I fear we are not getting rid of God because we still believe in grammar" (*TI*, 38) or "Rational thought is interpretation according to a scheme that we cannot cast off" (*KSA*, 12: 194), count among the standard references of the literature on Nietzsche. Yet these points had never before been made in a discourse like the one developed by Derrida; hence it seems appropriate to relate them to Nietzsche's text.

Among the postwar French writings about Nietzsche, Gilles Deleuze's 1962 study is exemplary for its radical break with the image of Nietzsche as a philosopher in the traditional sense.[3]

[1] See Josef Simon, "Grammatik und Wahrheit," *Nietzsche-Studien* 1 (1972): 1–27; and Karl Schlechta, "Nietzsche über den Glauben an die Grammatik," *Nietzsche-Studien* 1 (1972): 353–58.

[2] In a review in *Deutschland: Wochenschrift für Kunst, Literatur, Wissenschaft und soziales Leben* 46 (Aug. 16, 1890), 753–55. See also Elizabeth Bredeck, "Fritz Mauthners Nachlese zu Nietzsches Sprachkritik," *Nietzsche-Studien* 13 (1984): 586–99.

[3] Gilles Deleuze, *Nietzsche et la philosophie* (Paris: Presses Universitaires de France, 1962); idem, *Nietzsche and Philosophy*, trans. Hugh Tomlinson (New York: Columbia University Press, 1983).

The search for truth is replaced in Deleuze by interpretation, evaluation, and experimentation; in place of a topology of concepts, there emerges a topology of forces with changing, sliding forms of domination. The question of "What?" is replaced by the question "Who?" and answered with "Master," "Slave," and "Priest." Among the most impressive aspects of this text are doubtless the numerous powerful rejections of any trace of a dialectical method or dialectical meaning in Nietzsche. But Deleuze did not articulate his argument in the name of a theory of signs or with the help of such a theory.

Michel Foucault raised this theme, perhaps for the first time, in a paper on Nietzsche, Freud, and Marx presented at a philosophy conference in Royaumont in 1964 (*NFM*). Foucault sketched a hypothetical project of a universal encyclopedia covering all interpretive techniques from the Greek grammarians to the present day and outlined the particular chapter marked by Nietzsche, Freud, and Marx. Whereas the theory of signs and the techniques of interpretation in previous centuries are relatively clear, Foucault argued, the writings of Nietzsche, Marx, and Freud drive us into an "uncomfortable" hermeneutic situation. The interpretive techniques developed in *Capital, On the Genealogy of Morals,* and *The Interpretation of Dreams* have a shock effect: they outrage and affect us personally. Freud once said that there had been three "narcissistic" insults to Western culture: one produced by Copernicus, one caused by Darwin, and one caused by Freud himself. In this sense Marx, Nietzsche, and Freud entangle us in a process of interpretation that constantly reflects upon itself. They neither increased the number of signs nor created new meanings; rather, they changed the relationships among signs, ordered them in more complicated ways, placed mirrors among them, and thereby gave them new dimensions (*NFM*, 184).

Following these three, according to Foucault, interpretation has become an infinite task. The further we proceed, the nearer we approach a dangerous zone in which interpretation is not only rejected but disappears as interpretation and possibly draws interpreters with it. Foucault refers to Aphorism 39 from *Beyond Good and Evil*, in which Nietzsche said: "Indeed, it might be a basic characteristic of existence that those who would know it completely would perish" (*BGE*, 49). The actual reason, however, why interpretation does not end in this new situation is that the classical relation between the signifier and signified is no longer intact; it has become changeable or shifting. Foucault writes: "There is no longer anything foundational underlying interpretation; each sign that lends itself to interpretation is no longer the sign of an object, but already the interpretation of another sign" (*NFM*, 189).

Foucault draws attention to the first section of Nietzsche's *Genealogy of Morals* and its famous etymology of "good and evil" or "good and bad" and adds: "The words themselves are nothing but interpretations, throughout their entire history they interpret before they become signs, and in the end they signify only through their characteristics as signs." "Perhaps," he continues, "this primacy of interpretation over the sign is the decisive feature of modern hermeneutics" (*NFM*, 190). Foucault also suggests that since the nineteenth century the sign, with Marx, Nietzsche, and Freud, has become malicious and "hostile"; he refers in this regard to the functions of money for Marx, of the symptom for Freud, and of the values of good and evil for Nietzsche. This hermeneutics no longer believes in the absolute existence of signs but entangles itself within itself, in accordance with Nietzsche's assertion that there are only interpretations. For Nietzsche, in other words, hermeneutics and semiotics have become "bitter enemies," precisely because hermeneutics denies the existence of original signs (*NFM*, 192). Each sign, including that of language, each spoken word, is relevant only *as* interpretation—as an interpretation that we apply to an unknown and perhaps nonexistent text.

Another approach to Nietzsche's sign theory was suggested by Foucault in 1971 in the essay "Nietzsche, Genealogy, History" (*NGH*). Whereas history views events from the perspective of the endpoint, teleologically and with an anticipated meaning, genealogy concentrates on the contingency of events ("l'aléa singulier de l'événement"; "the singularity of events outside of any monotonous finality," *NGH*, 76), the episodes of history, the details and games of chance outside any preconceived finality (*NGH*, 76). Genealogy deals with "emergence," "origin," "descent," and "birth," in the sense of the origins of morality, asceticism, justice, or punishment (*NGH*, 77–78). In *The Gay Science* Nietzsche wrote: "All kinds of individual passions have to be thought through different ages, peoples, and great and small individuals; all their reason and all their evaluations and perspectives on things have to be brought to light. So far, all that has given color to existence still lacks a history" (*GS*, 81). Nietzsche then added the question: "Whatever men have so far viewed as the conditions of their existence—and all the reason, passion, and superstition involved in such a view—has this been researched exhaustively?" (*GS*, 82).

According to Foucault, such genealogical analyses by Nietzsche, particularly those in the *Genealogy of Morals*, reveal something completely different from the external appearance of things; for example, reason came into the world "by a chance accident" (*D*, 125); or the doctrine of the freedom of the will was "an invention of the *ruling* classes" (*KSA*, 2: 545). Such analyses demonstrate that there is no secret, atemporal essence of things lying behind them; their secret is that perhaps they have no essence, or that their essence is constructed piece by piece, out of forms foreign to them. As Foucault writes: "What is found at the historical beginning of things is not the inviolable identity of their origin; it is the dissension of other things. It is disparity" (*NGH*, 79). Analyses of origin and descent lead us further into a world in which we are ashamed and which we can only observe with horror.

Genealogy does not resemble the evolution of a species and does not map the destiny of a people. On the contrary, to follow the complex course of descent is to maintain passing events in their proper dispersion; it is to identify the accidents, the minute deviations—or conversely, the complete reversals—the errors, the false appraisals, and the faulty calculations which gave birth to those things that continue to exist and have value for us; it is to discover that truth or being does not lie at the root of what we know and what we are, but the exteriority of accidents.   (*NGH*, 81)

Undoubtedly these remarks move us into the terrain of those "signs without present truth," of which Derrida speaks in regard to Nietzsche. In order to emerge from Foucault's dark world, however, and to approach more closely Derrida's readings of Nietzsche, it is useful to consider some of the examples given by Nietzsche himself in his deconstructive semiology. An outstanding example is the analysis of punishment in the second essay of the *Genealogy of Morals*. According to Nietzsche, the "origin" of punishment must be carefully distinguished from its "purpose," although "they are usually confounded" (*GM*, 77). In a naive way, we generally begin by identifying a "purpose" in punishment, for example, revenge or intimidation, in order then to explain its origin. This is of a piece with viewing "the eye [as] being made for seeing, the hand being made for grasping" (*GM*, 77). In reality, however, "the cause of the origin of a thing and its eventual utility, its actual employment and place in a system of purposes, lie worlds apart" (*GM*, 77). Nietzsche argues that "whatever exists, having somehow come into being, is again and again reinterpreted to new ends, taken over, transformed, and redirected by some power superior to it" (*GM*, 77).

At this point, the hypothesis that in all such "fresh interpretations" a "will to power has become master of something less powerful and imposed upon it the character of a function" (*GM*, 77) should be set aside. For this would traduce Nietzsche's own interpretation and detract from the more fundamental discovery that "the entire history of a 'thing,' an organ, a custom," can be seen as a "continuous sign-chain of ever new interpretations and adaptations whose causes do not even have to be related to one another but, on the contrary, in some cases succeed and alternate with one another in a purely chance fashion" (*GM*, 77). Considered from the perspective of such a "genealogy," a phenomenon like punishment does not have one meaning "but a whole synthesis of 'meanings,'" which ultimately crystallize in "a kind of unity that is hard to disentangle, hard to analyze and, as must be emphasized especially, totally *indefinable*" (*GM*, 80). Nietzsche continues: "All concepts in which an entire process is semiotically concentrated elude definition; only that which has no history is definable" (*GM*, 80). Nietzsche undertook similar analyses of phenomena such as cruelty, pity, or conscience. Concerning revenge, he wrote: "The word 'revenge' is so quickly said: it almost appears that it could contain nothing but the root of a concept and an emotion. And we still tend to find the same: as our national economists do not tire of finding such a unity in the word 'value' and of searching for the original root concept of value. As if all words were not pouches, in which a little of this, a little of that, and a little of something else had suddenly been thrown" (*KSA*, 2: 564). In *The Gay Science*, Nietzsche says: "We have arranged for ourselves a world in which we can live—by positing bodies, lines, planes, causes and effects, motion and rest, form and content; without these articles of faith nobody now could endure life. But that does not prove them. Life is no argument. The conditions of life might include error" (*GS*, 177). After he has identified four errors, he concludes: "If we removed the effects of these four errors, we should also remove humanity, humaneness, and 'human dignity'" (*GS*, 174).

In the context of such analyses, Nietzsche makes assertions such as the following: "The total character of the world, however, is in all eternity chaos—in the sense not of a lack of necessity but of a lack of order, arrangement, form, beauty, wisdom, and whatever other names there are for our aesthetic anthropomorphisms" (*GS*, 168). The assumption of a world, which "is supposed to have its equivalent and its measure in human thought and human valuations—a 'world of truth' that can be mastered completely and forever with the aid of our square little reason," was for Nietzsche "a crudity and naiveté, assuming that it is not a mental illness, an idiocy" (*GS*, 335). Such a world is "not a factual case, but a poetic creation and rounding off of a meager sum of observations; it is 'in flux,' as something becoming, a constantly self-displacing falsity that never nears the truth, for: there is no 'truth'" (*KSA*, 12: 114).

These passages articulate Nietzsche's specific concept of interpretation, which Derrida argues consists in the gesture of "active interpretation." In one of his earliest writings, "On Truth and Lie in an Extra-Moral Sense" (1873), which he did not publish himself, Nietzsche outlined the concept of a sign fully separated from the concept of truth and thus involved in ongoing, active interpretation. His outline of a sign theory appears in his famous answer to the question "What is truth?": "A moving army of metaphors, metonymies, and anthropomorphisms, in short a summa of human relationships that are being poetically and rhetorically sublimated, transposed, and beautified until, after a long and repeated use, a people considers them solid, canonical, and unavoidable. Truths are illusions whose illusionary nature has been forgotten, metaphors that have been used up and have lost their imprint and that now operate as mere metal, no longer as coins" (*KSA*, 1: 880–81). In order to underline the complete contingency and constructedness of this human world of signs, to illustrate "how shadowlike and transitory, how purposeless and arbitrary the human intellect looks in nature," Nietzsche framed this text with the following fable: "In some faraway corner of the universe, hidden by countless twinkling solar systems, there was once a star on which clever animals invented knowledge. It was the proudest and most dishonest minute of 'world history'; but it lasted only a minute. After a few breaths of nature the star froze, and the clever animals had to die" (*KSA*, 1: 875).

The same fable appears almost word for word in "On the Pathos of Truth" (1872). This essay was also left unpublished by Nietzsche, but he had it bound in leather together with other texts from this time and, under the title "Five Prefaces to Five Unwritten Books," gave it as a Christmas gift in 1872 to Cosima Wagner (*KSA*, 14: 106). There the fable is told by an "unfeeling demon," and at the point when the clever animals die it continues: "It was also time: for, although they had already known much, boastfully, to their great embarrassment it was finally the case that they had learned falsely. They died and, while dying, cursed the truth. This was the manner of these desperate animals, the ones who had invented knowledge" (*KSA*, 1: 760).

Considered in the context of Nietzsche's early writings, these texts are of great interest, for they stem from about the same time in which he wrestled, as almost never again, with metaphysics, attempted to outdo Schopenhauer, and constructed a system in which he tried to derive the totality of beings from a single principle, the "primordial oneness."[4] The skeptical mode of reflection evident in these writings, already suggested in the notebooks of earlier years, became a position of linguistic and metaphysical critique.[5] It seems to represent the actual basis for the sudden end of Nietzsche's metaphysical experiments and thus has attracted the interest of those engaged in deconstructive readings of Nietzsche.[6]

It is unjustifiable, however, to draw this complex of critical fragments and writings out of Nietzsche's early texts as if it amounted to an assemblage, give it the title *The Philosopher's Book* (*Das Philosophenbuch*), and then juxtapose it as a critical,

[4]See Diana Behler, "Nietzsches Versuch einer Artistenmetaphysik," in *Kunst und Wissenschaft bei Nietzsche*, ed. Mihailo Djuric and Josef Simon (Würzburg: Könighausen, 1986), 130–49.

[5]Claudia Crawford, *The Beginning of Nietzsche's Theory of Language*, Monographs and Texts of Nietzsche Research, vol. 19 (Berlin: de Gruyter, 1988).

[6]Philippe Lacoue-Labarthe, "Le détour (Nietzsche et la rhétorique)," *Poétique* 2 (1971): 53–76; Paul de Man, "Rhetoric of Tropes (Nietzsche)," in idem, *Allegories of Reading: Figural Language in Rousseau, Nietzsche, Rilke and Proust* (New Haven: Yale University Press, 1976), 103–18.

skeptical text to the more metaphysical notes on "the artist's metaphysics" and *The Birth of Tragedy*.[7] This would repeat, though with the opposite intention, the fabrication or even falsification that led to *The Will to Power*.

Among the more effective reading techniques for these early writings is Paul de Man's search for a critical element within the metaphysical texts themselves, as opposed to transposing such an element from another body of texts.[8] Of course, this reading strategy would have to be supplemented by another, one that relates the metaphysically oriented texts of that time to the texts critical of metaphysics. Nietzsche had himself indicated the reciprocal crossing of these two discourses, when he said in the preface to the second part of *Human, All Too Human* that at the time of writing "Schopenhauer as Educator" (1874) he was "already in the midst of moral skepticism and dissolution": "precisely at this time arose a still secret writing 'on truth and lie in an extra-moral sense.'" His text "Richard Wagner in Bayreuth," despite its "appearance of 'actuality,'" would secretly be "an act of homage and gratitude for a piece of my past, the most beautiful and most dangerous stillness at sea of my journey ... in fact a separation, a taking leave" (*KSA*, 2: 370). At this point it is particularly important to note that Nietzsche's "On Truth and Lie in an Extra-Moral Sense" relies strongly on Gustav Gerber's *Language as Art* (1871).[9] The evidence shows that Nietzsche's early language

[7]Friedrich Nietzsche, *Das Philosophenbuch: Vorarbeiten zu einer Schrift über den Philosophen*, in idem, *Gesammelte Werke*, Musarionausgabe (Munich: Musarion, 1922), 6: 3–120.

[8]Paul de Man, "Rhetoric of Tropes (Nietzsche)" (cited in note 6 to this chapter), 117.

[9]Anthonie Meigers and Martin Stingelin, "Konkordanz zu den wörtlichen Abschriften und Übernahmen von Beispielen und Zitaten aus Gustav Gerber: *Die Sprache als Kunst* (Bromberg, 1871) in Nietzsches Rhetorik-Vorlesung und in 'Über Wahrheit und Lüge im außermoralischen Sinne,'" in *Nietzsche-Studien* 17 (1988): 350–68; Anthonie Meigers, "Gustav Gerber und Friedrich Nietzsche: Zum historischen Hintergrund der sprachphilo-

criticism closely followed the tendencies of German Romanticism and initially had an aesthetic-poetic interest.

In any case, Nietzsche's practice of "active interpretation" appears to consist in this reciprocal interaction of different types of interpretation, the deliberate exchange of perspectives. In one of his last writings, *Ecce Homo*, Nietzsche derived this concept of multiple interpretations from his experience of disease and decadence on the one hand and his immense healthiness on the other hand: "Looking from the perspective of the sick toward *healthier* concepts and values and, conversely, looking again from the fullness and self-assurance of a *rich* life down into the secret work of the instinct of decadence—in this I have had the longest training, my truest experience; if in anything, I became master in *this*. Now I know how, have the know-how, to *reverse perspectives*" (*GM*, 223).

In a letter to Carl Fuchs dated August 26, 1888, Nietzsche illustrated these practices with the apparently trivial example of an edition of musical manuscripts; he consequently held the position that in most cases what "is wrong" can be determined but what is right "almost never," and hence the assumption "that there is a correct, that is, one correct interpretation" is psychologically and experientially false (*KGB*, 5: 400). Nietzsche pointed to the situation of the composer in the act of creation, governed by chance and lability, and reached the conclusion: "In short, what the old philologist says on the basis of the entire philological experience: *there is no one true interpretation*, neither for poets, nor for musicians (a poet is absolutely no authority on the sense of his verses: we have the most miraculous evidence of how fluid and vague meaning is for them)" (*KGB*, 5: 400).

On the basis of his conviction that "forcing, adjusting, abbreviating, omitting, padding, inventing, falsifying" all belong

---

sophischen Auffassungen des frühen Nietzsche," in *Nietzsche-Studien* 17 (1988): 369–90. But see also Paul de Man, who stressed Gerber's importance for Nietzsche in *Allegories of Reading* (cited in note 6 to this chapter), 104–6.

to the "*essence* of interpretation" (*GM*, 151), Nietzsche saw the constant "reversal of perspective" (*BGE*, 44), that is, the persistent replacement of horizons by ever new ones, as entirely necessary. For him, the human being was the only one among all the animals for whom there are "no eternal horizons and perspectives" (*GS*, 192). Another important theme from the complex of "active interpretation," particularly in regard to Nietzsche's sense of the multiplicity of meaning, is the mask, which could be understood in the classical sense of *dissimulatio* as irony but also has the modern meaning of shame and self-defense, so that the unmasking has a tormenting, painful character.[10] In order to show the multiplicity of masks in interpretive practice through a relatively harmless example, we could cite the aphorism "On the garrulousness of writers," in which Nietzsche indicates the range of perspectives potentially hidden behind verbosity as a mask (*GS*, 150). He writes of the "garrulousness of wrath" in the cases of Luther and Schopenhauer, a "garrulousness due to a superabundant supply of conceptual formulations as in Kant," the "garrulousness due to the delight in ever new twists of the same thing," as in Montaigne, a "garrulousness due to the delight in good words and language forms" in Goethe's prose, or the "garrulousness due to an inner pleasure in noise and confused emotions: for example, in Carlyle" (*GS*, 150).

Nietzsche's active interpretation appears in a particularly dour form in the interpretation of philosophical works; he doubts the assumption that every philosopher "expressed his real and ultimate opinions in books" or the widespread idea that "whether behind every one of his caves there is not, must not be, another deeper cave—a more comprehensive, stranger, richer world beyond the surface, an abysmally deep ground behind every ground, under every attempt to furnish 'grounds'" (*BGE*, 229). Thus, in terms of his own writings,

[10]See the sections "The Free Spirit" and "What Is Noble?" in *BGE*, 35–56, 201–37.

Nietzsche often emphasized that he had reasons to "do everything to be 'hard to understand'" (*BGE*, 39) and granted his readers "from the outset some leeway and romping place for misunderstanding" (*BGE*, 40). In regard to the interpretation of moral and religious phenomena, his "active interpretation" often takes on masochistic elements (*BGE*, 44–45). But the most provocative act of this interpretation is doubtless the interpretation of the "ascetic ideal" and the "overcoming" of the ascetic ideal by the ascetic ideal itself, according to the motto: "All great things bring about their own destruction through an act of self-overcoming: thus the law of life will have it, the law of the necessity of 'self-overcoming' in the nature of life" (*GM*, 161).

Nietzsche's interpretation also turns on interpretation itself, when he asks which "intentions" underlie our commentaries and determine the "falsification of the facts of the case" (*BGE*, 24). One possible motive could be fear, as it appears in the interpretation of "inanimate things" while looking at the "sky, meadow, rocks, forest, storms, stars, sea, landscape, spring," whose friendly aspect would not appear "without the primeval habit, born of fear, of seeing behind all this a second, hidden meaning," or in other words, relating these things to the human world (*D*, 90). We would not now, he argued, "take pleasure in nature, just as we would take no pleasure in man and animal without this same instructor in understanding, fear" (*D*, 90).

The infinite interpretability of all things and processes leads directly to the question of "how far the perspective character of existence extends or indeed whether existence has any other character than this; whether existence without interpretation, without 'sense,' does not become 'nonsense'; whether, on the other hand, all existence is not essentially actively engaged in *interpretation*" (*GS*, 336). To be sure, Nietzsche admits, this is a question "that cannot be decided even by the most industrious and most scrupulously conscientious analysis and self-examination of the intellect" (*GS*, 336). For in the course of this analysis, the human intellect "cannot avoid seeing itself in its own perspectives, and only in these": "We cannot look around our own corner: it is a hopeless curiosity that wants to know what other kinds of intellects and perspectives there *might* be" (*GS*, 336). According to Nietzsche, however, we are at least "far from the ridiculous immodesty that would be involved in decreeing from our corner that perspectives are permitted only from this corner" (*GS*, 336). Instead, he writes, the world has

become "infinite" for us all over again, inasmuch as we cannot reject the possibility that *it may include infinite interpretations*. Once more we are seized by a great shudder; but who would feel immediately inclined to deify again this monster of an unknown world following the old manner? And to worship the unknown henceforth as "the Unknown One"? Alas, too many ungodly possibilities of interpretation are included in the unknown, too much devilry, stupidity, and foolishness of interpretation—even our own human, all too human folly, which we know.   (*GS*, 336–37)

Like the language criticism and the perspectivism of infinite interpretation, Nietzsche's conception of play—the play of the world, of art, and of philosophy—stemmed from Romanticism, though not in this case as much from Romanticism as it first emerged in Germany as from Romanticism as it later developed in France, particularly in the writings of Baudelaire, which Nietzsche studied closely at the time he was working on *Beyond Good and Evil*.[11] The crystallization for Nietzsche of the concept of play in the phrase *l'art pour l'art* indicates a French derivation, as Nietzsche himself believed. The concept, however, refers to the autonomy of the aesthetic, that disentanglement of art from all other contexts except art itself, which, following Kant's inspiration, became known as the freedom

---

[11] See Karl Pestalozzi, "Nietzsches Baudelaire-Rezeption," *Nietzsche-Studien* 7 (1978): 158–78; Mazzino Montinari, "Aufgaben der Nietzsche-Forschung heute: Nietzsches Auseinandersetzung mit der französischen Literatur des 19. Jahrhunderts," in *Nietzsche heute: Die Rezeption seines Werkes nach 1968*, Amherster Kolloquium 15, ed. Sigrid Bauschinger, Susan L. Cocalis, and Sara Lennox (Bern: Francke, 1988), 137–48.

from purpose of poetry, the pure play of literature, in the writings first of Friedrich Schlegel and then of Novalis.[12] Nietzsche himself was probably unaware of these connections. When, in the preface to the second edition of *The Gay Science*, he called for "another kind of art—a mocking, light, fleeting, divinely untroubled, divinely artificial art," and "above all, an art for artists, for artists only," he was more concerned with the concept of art that, he thought, had been developed in late French Romanticism and in the absolute or pure poetry of Symbolism.

The ample evidence confirming this claim includes some of Nietzsche's most scintillating statements and renders inconceivable any one-sided interpretation of his texts, especially those based on the theme of the will to power. As Nietzsche himself said, he was thinking of "the *late French Romanticism* of the forties" when he described the artists of l'art pour l'art as "these masters of new means of language," "these last great seekers," these "first artists steeped in world literature," these "mediators and mixers of the arts and senses":

all of them great discoverers in the realm of the sublime, also of the ugly and gruesome, and still greater discoverers concerning effects, display, and the art of display windows—all of them talents far beyond their genius—virtuosos through and through, with uncanny access to everything that seduces, allures, compels, overthrows; born enemies of logic and straight lines, lusting after the foreign, the exotic, the tremendous, the crooked, the self-contradictory.

(*BGE*, 197)

But Nietzsche also adduced Goethe, Beethoven, Heinrich Heine, and Richard Wagner as exemplars of this type; in a certain sense he drew this portrait to include himself as well. It is a question of that specific kind of artist he had described as "fanatics of *expression* 'at any price'" (*BGE*, 196–97).

[12]See Ernst Behler, "Nietzsche und die romantische Metaper von der Kunst als Spiel," in *Echoes and Influences of German Romanticism: Essays in Honor of Hans Eichner*, ed. Michael S. Batts, Anthony W. Riley, and Heinz Wetzel (Bern: Lang, 1987), 11–28.

It is important for the present discussion that Baudelaire stimulated Nietzsche's interest during the elaboration of these themes, and that at the time of this work Nietzsche made excerpts from Baudelaire's texts. Indeed, these excerpts contain much about Baudelaire's "poésie pure" (*KSA*, 13: 91) and his conception of beauty as something "glowing and sad" (*KSA*, 13: 79). These are also useful, however, to show the pessimism of decadence, "to become acquainted with it from the inside, through one who did not spare himself," and in whose decadence "the typically contemporary physiological weaknesses have found exemplary expression."[13] With this expression the phrase "l'art pour l'art" gains a variety of meanings. It suggests not only the will to create and the power of creation but also "aesthetic pessimism" (*KSA*, 12: 409) and nihilism (*KSA*, 12: 557). Such an art is accompanied by a range of beauties, which come into the world only through decadence.

The point is shown nowhere more clearly than in Aphorism 208 from *Beyond Good and Evil* on the "sickness of the will," Nietzsche's formulation for literary decadence (*BGE*, 130). Here he identifies France as "the school and display of all the charms of skepticism"—a quality that demonstrates its "cultural superiority over [the rest of] Europe"—because the French spirit has "always possessed a masterly skill at converting even the most calamitous turns of its spirit into something attractive and seductive" (*BGE*, 130). Nietzsche's reference to the conception of art as l'art pour l'art is even more explicit in the formulation: "and most of what today displays itself in the showcases, for example, as 'objectivity,' 'scientific,' 'l'art pour l'art,' 'pure knowledge, free of will,' is merely dressed-up skepticism and paralysis of the will: for this diagnosis of the European sickness I vouch" (*BGE*, 130).

Nietzsche illustrates the multiplicity of the concept of l'art pour l'art when he remarks: "The struggle against *purpose* in

[13] Karl Pestalozzi, "Nietzsches Baudelaire-Rezeption" (cited in note 11 to this chapter), 164–65.

art is always a struggle against the *moralizing* tendency in art, against the subordination of art to morality. L'art pour l'art means: 'the devil take morality!'" (*TI*, 81) In the same aphorism, however, he continues with the thought that, even "when one has excluded from art the purpose of moral preaching and human improvement," it does not at all follow "that art is completely purposeless, goalless, meaningless, in short l'art pour l'art—a snake biting its own tail" (*TI*, 81). Nietzsche pursues this thought further: "'Rather no purpose at all than a moral purpose!'—thus speaks mere passion. A psychologist asks on the other hand: what does all art do? does it not praise? does it not glorify? does it not select? does it not highlight? By doing all this it strengthens or weakens certain valuations" (*TI*, 81). The central thought underlying these particular reflections is that the "basic instinct" of artists is not necessarily directed toward art; rather it is directed toward life, "*towards the desirability of life*." The result of this reflection is contained in the sentence: "Art is the great stimulus to life: how could it be thought purposeless, aimless, *l'art pour l'art*?" (*TI*, 81)

This touches upon Nietzsche's deeply ambivalent understanding of art: on the one hand, art seems to him to be a completely purposeless, playful activity, yet on the other hand, it is an essentially purposeful, life-sustaining, and life-enhancing task. This duality in his understanding of art not only appears in different writings from the various phases of his life but is often condensed into a single concept, a single word, such as "decadence," about which he will make the most contradictory points in one and the same breath. If these different positions and analyses are followed in detail in Nietzsche's writings, it becomes evident that it is not art and poetry but rather thought, science, and philosophy in which, for Nietzsche, play finds its actual field of activity—although such a separation of art and science, poetry and philosophy, becomes *eo ipso* suspect with the inscription of play in philosophy. Nietzsche holds, however, to the letter of this distinction and gives to play a central position within philosophy, one that philosophy cannot occupy within poetry and art.

The view of philosophy as play appears, for example, in his characterization of the philosopher Heraclitus in the early text "Philosophy in the Tragic Age of the Greeks," in which Heraclitus assumes a thoroughly paradigmatic role for Nietzsche. As a person among people, Nietzsche writes, Heraclitus was "extraordinary." Even when he simply observed the play of noisy children, he "nevertheless thought of what no human had considered on such an occasion: the play of the great world-child Zeus" (*KSA*, 1: 834). In general, Heraclitus viewed the world from the perspective of the "aesthetic man," the philosopher "who had experienced through artists and the emergence of the work of art how the conflicts of multiplicity can nevertheless bring peace and law, how the artist stands above the work of art, observing and effective, just as necessity and play, conflict and harmony, must join to produce a work of art" (*KSA*, 1: 831). In this world, "only the play of the artist and the child" builds and destroys "without any moral evaluation," with an "eternally indifferent innocence" (*KSA*, 1: 830). The philosopher had no reason, as had, for example, Leibniz, to prove that the world is the best of all possible places: "It satisfied him that the world is the beautiful, innocent play of the age" (*KSA*, 1: 830). And thus, Nietzsche concludes, that which Heraclitus viewed as "the doctrine of the law of becoming and of play in necessity" (*KSA*, 1: 835) should be "viewed eternally: he had lifted the curtain on this great drama" (*KSA*, 1: 835).

The centrality of the play concept for Nietzsche's philosophy can be seen in the images of the playing child and of the "fairy tales and play" accompanying every age (*KSA*, 2: 493). It is announced in the description of the "eternal comedy of existence" and the "waves of uncountable laughter" (*GS*, 75), and in the conception of the "gay science" as "la gaya scienza" (*GS*, 33). It is expressed in the movement of the dance and the game of the world, as in the verses:

World game, the ruling force,
blends false and true:
the eternally fooling force
blends us in too.
    (*GS*, 351)

These lines clearly express the character of play in Nietzsche's philosophy and poetry. His writings appear as "the expression of an intellectual play impulse, and innocent and happy like all play" (*GS*, 170), as the communications of a playful spirit: "the ideal of a spirit who plays naively—that is, not deliberately but from overflowing power and abundance—with all that was hitherto called holy, good, untouchable, divine" (*GS*, 347).

Nietzsche's "style," which corresponds to his basic philosophical orientation and according to Derrida is of a multiple or "plural" form, refers not only to his literary production and form of writing but also to his views of art and life in general. From this perspective his central philosophical themes appear in a new light. If the truth claim is dismissed in the treatment of these themes, then they can be treated in ways that illustrate their practical consequences for life and being in the world. Perhaps it was Nietzsche's intention to free us from the engrained need to develop epistemological theories, moral structures, and ontological systems as a way of justifying our statements, answers, and life practices.[14]

From this angle, the question of Nietzsche's perspective would not amount to an epistemological theory, which would be difficult to maintain because of the problem of self-reference. Nietzsche's tropes of "truth" and "error," "fact" and "interpretation," amount instead to rhetorical devices, designed to help us see our prejudicial belief that there must be a final truth on which to build our morality. The *Übermensch* would not, in this view, offer a prescriptive model of human

---

[14]See Bernd Magnus, "Perfectibility and Attitude in Nietzsche's *Übermensch*," *Review of Metaphysics* 36 (1983): 633–59.

self-completion and self-overcoming; rather, he would present or make visible an attitude toward life that has overcome nihilism and *ressentiment*, and sees life and the world as worthy of infinite repetition. The fact that Nietzsche left the concept of *Übermensch* relatively vague and indeterminate is not an indication of weakness in this perspective but a stylistic and linguistic achievement, since theoretically every *Übermensch* should realize himself in his own way. The "will to power" would constitute not a doctrine but a recommendation to replace the thought of things by the representation of events or sequences of events, that is, by genealogy, in which the sequences of events would be fully contingent and consist in constantly changing interpretations.[15] As Nietzsche wrote: "Judgments, value judgments concerning life, for or against, can in the last resort never be true: they possess value only as symptoms, they come into consideration only as symptoms" (*TI*, 30).

To take only one of the major themes of Nietzsche's philosophy and to illustrate the difficulty of making a final determination and "binding" statements, it is useful to consider Nietzsche's term "Socratism" in his early writings. The term seems to inscribe a distinctly circumscribed complex of meanings.[16] In Aphorism 15 of *The Birth of Tragedy*, Nietzsche had introduced Socratism as "a shadow that keeps growing in the evening sun," one that has spread over the entire world creating a "profound *illusion*"—namely, "the unshakable faith that thought, using the thread of causality, can penetrate the deepest abysses of being, and that thought is capable not only of knowing being but even of *correcting* it" (*BT*, 95). As for the connection between this scientific, optimistic type of thought

---

[15] It becomes clear here that Bernd Magnus argues both from the position of Derrida's deconstruction and in the sense of Rorty's pragmatism. See esp. Magnus, *Nietzsche's Existential Imperative* (Bloomington: Indiana University Press, 1978).

[16] See Ernst Behler, "Sokrates und die griechische Tragödie: Nietzsche und die Brüder Schlegel über den Ursprung der Moderne," *Nietzsche-Studien*, special issue: "Gedenkband für Mazzino Montinari," 18 (1989): 141–57.

and art, Nietzsche adds: "This sublime metaphysical illusion accompanies science as an instinct and leads science again and again to its limits at which it must turn into *art—which is really the aim of this mechanism*" (*BT*, 95–96). Underlying this position is the idea that the infinite desire for knowledge will inevitably be shipwrecked. In Socrates, "the hunger for insatiable and optimistic knowledge" moves irresistibly toward its own limits, attempts to survey the boundaries of science, and then recognizes "how logic coils up at these boundaries and finally bites its own tail" (*BT*, 98). At these points, insatiable knowledge turns abruptly into "tragic resignation and the destitute need for art" (*BT*, 98). Here a "new form of insight" breaks through: "*tragic insight* which, merely to be endured, needs art as a protection and remedy" (*BT*, 98). But this final reversal of science and philosophy into tragic insight and the need for art, embodied in the image of the "*Socrates who practices music*" (*BT*, 98), lies beyond typical Socratism and carries out its self-overcoming. By contrast, for Nietzsche the historically prototypical character of the philosopher is marked by the optimism of theoretical knowledge. With Socrates, Nietzsche argues, Western culture embarked on a journey that must shipwreck on the rocks of tragic insight.

At this point the primary issue is the impact of Socratism, which according to Nietzsche brought about the essential dissolution of the classical Greek ideal of life. The main witness testifying to this change is Euripides, who, according to Nietzsche and also to Aristophanes, attended the school of Socrates and transposed his lessons to the stage as a form of "aesthetic Socratism." The Athenian public had previously possessed a keen sense for the aura of incomprehensibility surrounding "Aeschylean-Sophoclean tragedy" (*BT*, 84), whose effects derived from pathos, from "the great rhetorical-lyrical scenes in which the passion and dialectic of the protagonist swelled to a broad and powerful current" (*BT*, 84). From the Socratic principle, the idea that "knowledge is virtue," the law of "aesthetic Socratism" became "To be beautiful everything must be intelligible" (*BT*, 83–84). The result was a species of Greek tragedy as a chess-like game, which continued in Attic comedy and which initiated the phase of modernity in literature.

If we look more closely for the decisive moment of the dissolution of classical antiquity and the classical ideal, however, it appears that the concept of Socratism is highly unstable. For, Nietzsche argues, in order to measure the impact of the Socratic character, anyone who has experienced the Platonic writings would also have to feel "how the enormous driving-wheel of logical Socratism is in motion, as it were, *behind* Socrates, and that it must be viewed through Socrates as through a shadow" (*BT*, 88–89). Socrates appears, then, as the "representative of an 'anti-Dionysian tendency,'" which operated even before and through him and "merely received in him an unprecedentedly magnificent expression" (*BT*, 92). This impression is strengthened if we consider more closely the process of dissolution of classical tragedy achieved by "aesthetic Socratism" or "Euripideanism": here, too, it becomes clear that this process did not begin with Euripides but in a much earlier disparity between the "Athenian public" and classical tragedy (*KSA*, 1: 537).

Thus "Socratism" is "older than Socrates" (*KSA*, 1: 545); the aesthetic dissolution of tragedy had begun to appear "long before Euripides" and was already evident in Sophocles (*KSA*, 1: 548). More specifically, it begins to appear with the dialogue, which did not exist "in tragedy originally" and which consequently led to "debate," "competition," "disputes"—in a word: dialectics—and set in motion a process that led to "the drama of intrigue" (*KSA*, 1: 545–46). To make the point perhaps more radically, since the spatiotemporalizing manner of existence in which Nietzsche finds the basis for the collapse of classical antiquity had already appeared in the original music and dance of tragedy, there never was a true classicism. Nietzsche was understood in this way by his friend Heinrich Romundt, who, after reading the text "Socrates and Tragedy," wrote in 1870 that he found it "masterful how you proceed from Euripides, whose manner you investigate and represent without haste, then you sublimate the concept of Euripideanism into that of Socratism, and finally you demonstrate that Socratism was a pre- and post-Socratic—that is to say, eternal—disease" (*KGB* II, 2: 176). To state the point more exactly: the concept of "the classical" (in the sense of an exemplary) ideal, or objectively valid moment, can be maintained only by a reductionist reading of these texts and immediately begins to dissolve under closer scrutiny.

This is one specific example of Nietzsche's plurality of styles; it could also be illustrated by a number of other instances outside the concerns of philosophical epistemology or philological-historical research. With such artistry, Nietzsche hoped to have reached "that art of nuances which constitutes the best gain of life" and which allows us to distance ourselves from "the taste for the unconditional," for Nietzsche "the worst of tastes" (*BGE*, 43). For after one has "assaulted men and things in this manner with Yes and No," one should try "to put a little art into his feelings and rather to risk trying even what is artificial—as the real artists of life do" (*BGE*, 43).

Epicurus is an example of a mature artist of life from antiquity. He represents for Nietzsche "the happiness of the afternoon of antiquity": "I see his eyes gaze upon a wide, white sea, across rocks at the shore that are bathed in sunlight, while large and small animals are playing in this light, as secure and calm as the light and his eyes" (*GS*, 110). As he, however, describes the Epicurean art of life further, Nietzsche continues: "Such happiness could be invented only by a man who was suffering continually. It is the happiness of eyes that have seen the sea of existence become calm, and now they can never weary of the surface and of the many hues of this tender, shuddering skin of the sea. Never before has voluptuousness been so modest" (*GS*, 110). In the modern world, "the 'good Europeans'" (*BGE*, 195), those "fanatics of *expression* 'at any price'" (*BGE*, 197)—figures like Goethe, Balzac, Beethoven, Stendhal, Heine, Baudelaire, Delacroix, Schopenhauer, and Richard Wagner—represent the artists of living in the world. All were broken people, every one of them decadents lamed by the sickness of the will (*BGE*, 130–31), but nevertheless "on the whole, an audaciously daring, magnificently violent type of higher human beings who soared, and tore others along, to the heights—it fell to them first to teach their century—and it is the century of the *crowd*!—the concept 'higher man'" (*BGE*, 197).

When he returns to the model of classical antiquity, in the preface to the second edition of *The Gay Science*, Nietzsche describes it as the highest achievement by the Greeks in the art of life, as he concludes a long meditation on the topic:

Oh, those Greeks! They knew how to live. What is required for that is to stop courageously at the surface, the fold, the skin, to adore appearance, to believe in forms, tones, words, in the whole Olympus of appearance. Those Greeks were superficial—out of profundity. And is not this precisely what we are again coming back to, we dare-devils of the spirit who have climbed the highest and most dangerous peak of present thought and looked around from up there—we who have looked *down* from there? Are we not, precisely in this respect, Greeks? Adorers of forms, of tones, of words? And therefore—*artists*?   (*GS*, 38)

These reflections lead directly to Nietzsche's use of masks, dissimulation, and irony, which are among the most suggestive features not only of his doctrine of life as art but also of his theory of signs in general.[17] Toward the end of Aphorism 40 in *Beyond Good and Evil*, a particularly important passage for this topic (it begins "Whatever is profound loves masks"), Nietzsche says regarding the tactic for life and communication of "a concealed man" that he "instinctively needs speech for silence and for burial in silence" and "is inexhaustible in his evasion of communication" (*BGE*, 51). According to Nietz-

[17]See Ernst Behler, "Nietzsches Auffassung der Ironie," *Nietzsche-Studien* 4 (1975): 1–35; Walter Kaufmann, "Nietzsches Philosophie der Masken," *Nietzsche-Studien* 10/11 (1981/82): 111–31. See also *DTM*, 137–66.

sche, such a man wants and demands "that a mask of him roams in his place through the hearts and heads of his friends" (*BGE*, 51). But even if he did not want it, "he would still realize some day that in spite of that a mask of his is there—and that this is well" (*BGE*, 51). For, Nietzsche argues, "Every profound spirit needs a mask: even more, around every profound spirit a mask is growing continually, owing to the constantly false, namely *shallow*, interpretation of every word, every step, every sign of life he gives" (*BGE*, 51).

To see the sharp contradiction between Heidegger's and Derrida's images of Nietzsche, it is necessary only to recall Heidegger's very different comments on Nietzsche's "grand style" (*N*, 2: 11–13). For Heidegger, this style offered a program for the planetary domination of the earth with racial breeding, the operational and controlled manipulation of all beings, the simplification of all things and people into a manageable unity, total planetary mechanization by a new caste of masterminds. The fact that Heidegger glimpsed an ideal in such developments relates to his contemporary belief in technology (1937). Of course, the objection might be raised that the pertinent text for Heidegger addresses the realm of political and military forms of dominion, or the domination of the earth, whereas the text from *Beyond Good and Evil* deals with the aesthetic discipline of self-mastery. But Heidegger also treats this aesthetic aspect of Nietzsche's writings under the rubric of "the grand style" (*N*, 1: 124) and, in this instance too, reaches the opposite conclusions: "The artistic states are—and that means art is—nothing else than *will to power*. Now we understand Nietzsche's principal declaration concerning art as the great 'stimulant of life.' 'Stimulant' means what conducts one into the sphere of command of the grand style" (*N*, 1: 130).

An important reason for these differences of interpretation undoubtedly lies in the fact that for Heidegger, when dealing with nearly every topic of Nietzsche's writings, the "*sole concern is to know the basic position of Nietzsche's thought*" (*N*, 1: 131), which he interprets in most cases as "metaphysical." For

example, regarding Nietzsche's aesthetics, or indeed in relation
to every "true aesthetics," Heidegger explains his kind of interpretation accordingly: "At first glance, Nietzsche's thinking
concerning art is aesthetic; according to its innermost will, it is
metaphysical, which means it is a definition of the Being of
beings. The historical fact that every true aesthetics—for example, the Kantian—explodes itself is an unmistakable sign
that, although the aesthetic inquiry into art does not come
about by accident, it is not what is essential" (*N*, 1: 131).

This tendency appears as well in Heidegger's interpretation
of book titles like *The Gay Science* (*Die fröhliche Wissenschaft*),
which, as Nietzsche indicated by the subtitle *la gaya scienza*,
stems from an old European tradition expressed by the *gai
saber* of the troubadours and connected by Nietzsche to an
author as far removed as Emerson.[18] But none of this is found
in Heidegger's explanation; he argues that the concept of "science" in the title means "*the stance adopted, and the will directed, toward essential knowing*" (*N*, 2: 20). The "gaiety mentioned here" is not the "superficiality of fleeting enjoyment,"
but "a cheerfulness that is not dashed by even the hardest and
most terrifying matters. In the realm of knowing, cheerfulness
is not frightened by such things, but is rather invigorated by
them, inasmuch as cheerfulness affirms the necessity of these
most questionable things" (*N*, 2: 21). Once again Nietzsche is
driven into a metaphysical position that in this case seems especially at odds with the motif of "gay science."

Yet the point here is not to criticize Heidegger's image of
Nietzsche but to raise a more difficult question: How do those
texts by Nietzsche, which Heidegger uses as the basis for his
argument, relate to the deconstructive readings of Nietzsche
in which everything appears as an ungrounded play of signs?
This problem can by no means be brushed aside by the dismis-

[18]In the epigraph to the 1882 edition (*GS*, 27). Kaufmann (*GS*, 7–13)
gives the source of this quotation in his introduction to the translation.

---

sive reply that Heidegger's textual evidence, for the most part derived from the compilation *The Will to Power*, considers only an astoundingly small number of fragments. Evidence for Heidegger's arguments can be found among Nietzsche's published writings. Even such a subtle aphorism as the one concerning the "sickness of the will" in late nineteenth-century Europe ends with the statement: "The time for petty politics is over: the very next century will bring the fight for the dominion of the earth—the *compulsion* to large-scale politics" (*BGE*, 131). To direct this struggle into the right hands, Nietzsche recommends that "a new caste" should "rule Europe," one with "a long, terrible will of its own that would be to cast its goals millennia hence" (*BGE*, 131).

Such passages are plentiful in Nietzsche's writings. Heidegger stated that, for example, the aphorism on the "blond beast" (*GM*, 40) is not an isolated and extravagant statement in Nietzsche's text. In *Ecce Homo* Nietzsche looks "ahead a century" with the assumption that if his "attempt to assassinate two millennia of antinature and desecration of man were to succeed," a new form of life "would tackle the greatest of all tasks, the attempt to raise humanity higher, including the relentless destruction of everything that was degenerating and parasitical," and "would again make possible that excess of life on earth from which the Dionysian state, too, would have to awaken again" (*GM*, 274). A similar thought appears in the unpublished fragments. "International sexual organizations" will emerge with the task "of breeding a race of masters, the future 'masters of the earth'—a new, monstrous aristocracy, built on the hardest self-discipline, philosophical men of violence and artist-tyrants given power by the will to endure for over a thousand years" (*KSA*, 12: 87).

The question remains of how to reconcile such statements with the self-critical and more ironic texts by Nietzsche highlighted in deconstructive readings. A possible answer is suggested by Richard Rorty, who argues that the vocabulary of philosophers like Nietzsche should be divided into a largely private, ironic, self-critical sector and a smaller public, political sector, with absolutely no relation between the two. The personal value judgments of such philosophers should be seen as extraordinary and could perhaps help us to create alternative visions of ourselves, for they encourage us to write a new *Bildungsroman* about our old selves. But if one then presumes to judge "modern society," "the destiny of Europe," or contemporary politics from such a perspective, it becomes "at best vapid, and at worst sadistic" (*CIS*, 120). To be sure, this argument relies on Rorty's dismissal of philosophy for the purposes of "social engineering" and amounts essentially to saying that Nietzsche's paroxysms in this area merely underline the uselessness of philosophers and the irrelevance of philosophy for the treatment of social questions.

The depoliticization of Nietzsche had in fact already occurred in the North American reception following World War II. It is most apparent, though based on an entirely different argument, in the writings of Walter Kaufmann on Nietzsche.[19] Kaufmann, whose interpretation of Nietzsche was enormously influential in the English-speaking world, suggested that the will to power was to be understood outside the political-social sphere. With this bracketing of the concept, he portrayed the will to power as an apolitical principle of personal, existential self-overcoming and self-transcendence. In such a perspective, Nietzsche is not a political thinker, and we should not search in his writings for a political philosophy. Like Kierkegaard he focused on the individual, and his real strength was in the discussion of personal development and self-mastery.

Indeed, Rorty's argument seems to have a certain similarity to Kaufmann's, although the two recommendations for the de-

[19] See *NPPA*. A complete picture of Kaufmann's influence on the study of Nietzsche in North America can emerge only through a consideration of his translations of Nietzsche, which are accompanied by introductions and commentaries. See the Translator's Afterword to the present volume for a further discussion of the reception of Nietzsche in English.

politicization of Nietzsche, or a depoliticized reading of Nietzsche, proceed from entirely different presuppositions. This depoliticized reading of Nietzsche, however, above all in the reaction to Kaufmann's work, produced a lively controversy in which the question of the relation between Nietzsche's various texts and his "styles" re-emerged.

In 1979 J. P. Stern published *A Study of Nietzsche*, which, in Walter H. Sokel's words, "brought back the embarrassingly political Nietzsche that Kaufmann's influence had almost allowed us to forget." [20] Despite his high regard for Kaufmann's achievement, Sokel drew attention to the "antiseptic image" created and saw, in the elimination of the political model of domination and the pure "aestheticism" of these forms of domination, the most serious weakness in Kaufmann's interpretation. Much earlier, during World War II, Crane Brinton had made the distinction between the "gentle" and the "tough" interpreters of Nietzsche.[21] Seen from the perspective of the contemporary controversy, "gentle" interpreters would be those who take Nietzsche's statements metaphorically and interpret the will to power as self-overcoming; "tough" interpreters would be those who point to the connections between Nietzsche and Hitler or who raise the topic of Nietzsche and the Jews anew.[22]

To be sure, this is not a particularly productive distinction, because such interpretations analyze Nietzsche's texts primarily under the assumption of a likely "proto-fascism." It would

[20] J. P. Stern, *A Study of Nietzsche* (Cambridge, Eng.: Cambridge University Press, 1979). Walter H. Sokel, "Political Uses and Abuses of Nietzsche in Walter Kaufmann's Image of Nietzsche," *Nietzsche-Studien* 12 (1983): 441.

[21] Crane Brinton, *Nietzsche* (Cambridge, Mass.: Harvard University Press, 1941).

[22] Peter Heller, "Concerning the Nietzsche Cult and Literary Cults Generally," in *Nietzsche: Literature and Values*, ed. Volker Dürr, Reinhold Grimm, Kathy Harms (Madison: University of Wisconsin Press, 1988), 199–218; Peter Heller, "Nietzsche and the Jews," in *Nietzsche heute* (cited in note 11 to this chapter).

seem necessary and appropriate, however, both to consider his texts in terms of their entirety, and to analyze each one in detail as to its particular qualities. It appears once more that Derrida has a response to this question, insofar as the problem of textuality stands in the foreground of his reading of Nietzsche.

◁□▷

4

Derrida/Nietzsche

For Derrida, the first opportunity to give a comprehensive presentation of his Nietzsche was the colloquium at Cerisy-la-Salle in July 1972. The colloquium was organized under the provocative title of "Nietzsche Today?" ("Nietzsche aujourd'hui?"),[1] and according to Maurice de Gandillac, some participants turned "more and more to the contributions of the new linguistics and 'deconstructive' textual readings" for their interpretations of Nietzsche.[2] In reference to recent works on Nietzsche by Sarah Kofman, Philippe Lacoue-Labarthe, Bernard Pautrat, and Jean-Michel Rey, Derrida indicated at the outset that his own reflections would move in "that space which certain readings, in launching a new phase in the process of deconstructive (i.e. affirmative) interpretation, have demarcated during the last two years."[3]

Derrida gave his lecture the title "Nietzsche's Styles" be-

[1] The proceedings were published as *Nietzsche aujourd'hui?*, 2 vols. (Paris: Union Générale d'Editions, 1974).

[2] Maurice de Gandillac, "Le Colloque de Cerisy-la-Salle," *Nietzsche-Studien* 4 (1975): 324.

[3] Jacques Derrida, "Eperons. Les styles de Nietzsche," from vol. 1 of *Nietzsche aujourd'hui?* (cited in note 1 to this chapter), has appeared in numerous single editions and translations. In German the text appears in the volume *Nietzsche aus Frankreich* (cited in note 1 to the Introduction), 129–68. For an English translation, see *SNS*.

cause it explicitly demonstrates the critical points of his reading
of Nietzsche: the absence of any sign fully present in truth,
active deciphering, the affirmation of the world as play, and
the concept of style as plural. A further incentive for this title,
particularly the choice of the plural "styles," doubtlessly arose
from the publication of Heidegger's lectures on Nietzsche;
these had just appeared in France, and from the beginning the
lecture series on "The Will to Power as Art" had emphasized
"the grand style" in the singular. The title image of *Spurs*, related to the pen, the stiletto, the knife, and even the umbrella,
suggests the driving, penetrating features of Nietzsche's writing that turn variously against presence, veiling essence, meaning, and truth. Derrida's central argument, however, links
Nietzsche's styles to the theme of woman in his writings, and
hence the discussion of truth—style—woman forms an inter-
connecting complex. These interconnections give the lecture
an ironic, playful, frivolous character from the outset, a tone
that corresponds to its argument.

The text itself is composed in that "expository" style familiar from "La Différance." It follows no linear progression in
its presentation, avoids any ordering of evidence, and rejects
all strategies oriented toward an eventual purpose, as well
as all teleological tactics as they are most often found in
philosophical-logical discourse. It simply dramatizes its theme:
Nietzsche, Nietzsche's styles, Nietzsche's truth, Nietzsche's
text. To be sure, this lecture goes far beyond "La Différance"
in its audacity and innovation; perhaps, then, it is not the
best example for a critical analysis, which is typically inter-
ested more in direct statements than in the techniques of indirect communication. As Friedrich Schlegel aptly remarked:
"Nothing suffers commentary less willingly or avenges itself
against commentary more bitterly than a product of wit."

Derrida was well aware that Nietzsche's text in general is
dominated by a "venomous anti-feminism," with which the
few "*apparently feminist* propositions" he has found cannot
easily be reconciled (*SNS*, 57). More precisely: it is difficult to

determine Nietzsche's stance regarding this issue; Nietzsche's own exposition thus parallels the image of woman Nietzsche constructs in his texts. For Nietzsche, woman is in general a mysterious, allegorical figure that represents life, truth, style, and many other things but possesses no definable identity, no ontological essence. The figure resists understanding and does not reveal "her grounds" (*GS*, 38). Nietzsche's woman is a puzzle, a simulacrum, who presides over *actio in distans*, has an impact at a distance, seduces from afar through style and non-cognitive means.

Derrida refers at this point to Aphorism 60 of *The Gay Science*, in which Nietzsche describes the mentality of a young enthusiast who, surrounded by the "flaming surf" of the ocean, sees "a large sailboat, gliding along as silently as a ghost," and is gripped by a strange magic, as if "all the calm and taciturnity of the world" had "embarked on it" (*GS*, 123). "It seems," Nietzsche concludes the parable, "as if the noise here had led me into fantasies. All great noise leads us to move happiness into some quiet distance" (*GS*, 123). In this way, he continues, "when a man stands in the midst of his own noise," or "in the midst of his own surf of plans and projects," he sees in woman "his better self," stillness, and dreams. There is, however, "even on the most beautiful sailboat . . . a lot of noise, and unfortunately much small and petty noise" (*GS*, 124), such that the effect, then, is a long-distance one, which requires "first of all and above all—*distance*" (*GS*, 124).

Nietzsche characterizes another illusionary effect with the figure of woman and the gesture of concealment or masking. Derrida describes it as "the complicity (rather than the unity) between woman, life, seduction, modesty—all the veiled and veiling effects" (*SNS*, 51). In this context the woman seems synonymous with life, as Nietzsche himself had indicated in the aphorism "Vita femina" from *The Gay Science*: "I mean to say that the world is overfull of beautiful things but nevertheless poor, very poor when it comes to beautiful moments and unveilings of these things. But perhaps this is the most powerful magic of life: it is covered by a veil interwoven with gold, a veil of beautiful possibilities, sparkling with promise, resistance, bashfulness, mockery, pity, and seduction. Yes, life is a woman" (*GS*, 271–72).

Above all, however, truth is a woman for Nietzsche, as he suggested in the preface to *Beyond Good and Evil* and in many other passages; that is, it/she is an essence that does not allow itself to be taken in and of which it can be said "that she has not allowed herself to be won" (*BGE*, 2). More precisely, since the argument is that there is no truth, woman is only the name for "that untruth of truth" (*SNS*, 51). This had not always been the case. In his famous "'History of an error': How the 'true world' became a fable," Nietzsche tells how truth was initially an idea and that Plato said, "I, Plato, *am* the truth" (*TI*, 40). But this changed in the course of time. Truth became the problem of the non-presence of truth, that is, a woman, and now only the "credulous and dogmatic" (*SNS*, 53) philosopher believes in truth and in women. But for Nietzsche it is not only that he "has been very inexpert about women" (*BGE*, 2), but also that he has understood nothing. To cite Derrida: "He has understood nothing of truth, nor anything of woman. Because, indeed, if woman *is* truth, *she* at least knows that there is no truth, that truth has no place here and that no one has a place for truth. And she is woman precisely because she herself does not believe in truth itself, because she does not believe in what she is, in what she is believed to be, in what she thus is not" (*SNS*, 53).

Through this veiled, playful treatment of truth and women, Derrida ironically dramatizes several important ideas about Nietzsche, his styles, his texts, and his truths. The distance required for the effect of woman (truth) seems to create an opening for truth, but truth (woman) disappears in it: "Out of the depths, endless and unfathomable, she engulfs and distorts all vestige of essentiality, of identity, of property. And the philosophical discourse, blinded, founders on these shoals and is hurled down these depthless depths to its ruin. There is no such thing as the truth of woman, but it is because of that abyssal divergence of the truth, because that untruth is 'truth'" (*SNS*, 51).

Derrida's argument could be read as a feminist one and indeed, with varying emphases, has been read as such. In this perspective the dissolution of truth as woman would eliminate the fixation on the truth of woman derived from Platonic (or Rousseauistic) metaphysics and the "phallogocentric" tradition in general (*SNS*, 97). This is an important point, for it means that "'Woman'—her name made epoch—no more believes in castration's exact opposite, anti-castration, than she does in castration itself" (*SNS*, 61). Here lies woman's deepest skepticism, expressed by Nietzsche in his own way in Aphorism 64 of *The Gay Science*: "I am afraid that old women are more skeptical in their most secret of hearts than any man: they consider the superficiality of existence its essence, and all virtue and profundity is to them merely a veil over this 'truth,' a very welcome veil over a pudendum—in other words, a matter of decency and shame, and no more than that" (*GS*, 125). For Derrida, this passage suggests that "woman" does not believe in the profundity or the truth of the castration effect but "amuses herself [*en joue*] with it" (*SNS*, 61). In amusing herself with veils, she joins forces with artifice and the artist; her "histrionic capacity" also brings her closer to the Jews, who exercise their power with a similar "delight in dissimulation" (*SNS*, 69). At this point Derrida explores a number of associations, supported by some of the most suggestive passages from Nietzsche; these give a better impression of Derrida's reading of Nietzsche than could any theoretical analysis of his writing (*SNS*, 69–71).

The next question involves the "interpretation of Nietzsche's text," the question "of the interpretation of interpretation," or of interpretation itself (*SNS*, 73). This question appears, according to Derrida, when it "pierces the veil of truth and the simulacrum of castration in order to impale the woman's body" (*SNS*, 71). Here the question of interpretation must either be resolved or be disqualified as incapable of expression

(*SNS*, 73). This question, however, finds its sharpest provocation in what Derrida calls Nietzsche's "heterogeneity of the text" (*SNS*, 95). Nietzsche had no illusion that he knew what the "effects called woman, truth, castration, nor of those *ontological* effects of present and absence" consist in (*SNS*, 95). But he protected himself from the mere disavowal of valid statements and did not, therefore, write a "simple discourse against castration and its system," but used "discrete parody," the "strategy of writing," the "difference or deviation in quills"; in a word: the "heterogeneity of the text" (*SNS*, 95). Precisely this heterogeneity of the text "poses the limit to the relevance of the hermeneutic or systematic question" and "describes a margin where the control over meaning or code is without recourse" (*SNS*, 99).

This does not necessarily derive from Nietzsche's "mastery," nor does it follow that his "power" is "impregnable, or his manipulation of the snare impeccable. One cannot conclude, in order to outmaneuver the hermeneutic hold, that his is an infinite calculus which ... is similar to that of Leibniz' God. Such a conclusion, in its very attempt to elude the snare, succumbs all the more surely to it" (*SNS*, 99). For this would then only reconstitute "parody or the simulacrum as a weapon in the service of truth or castration," "as a Nietzsche cult for example," or a "priesthood of parody interpreters (*prêtrise de l'interprête es parodies, interprêtrise*)" (*SNS*, 99). Derrida takes a skeptical view: "This inability to assimilate—even among themselves—the aphorisms and the rest—perhaps it must simply be admitted that Nietzsche himself did not see his way too clearly there. No[r] could he, in the instantaneous blink of an eye. Rather a regular, rhythmic blindness takes place in the text. One will never have done with it" (*SNS*, 101). To Derrida, Nietzsche seems "a little lost in the web of his text, lost much as a spider who finds he is unequal to the web he has spun" (*SNS*, 101). In any case, for Nietzsche, "there is no such thing as a woman, as a truth in itself of woman in itself" (*SNS*, 101). This is confirmed by the "manifold typology of women in his work, its horde of mothers, daughters, sisters, old maids, wives, governesses, prostitutes, virgins, grandmothers, big and little girls" (*SNS*, 103).

For this reason, however, "there is no such thing either as the truth of Nietzsche, or of Nietzsche's text," according to Derrida (*SNS*, 103). Even when he speaks for himself, truth is "multiple" for him and, merely, "*my* truths" (*BGE*, 162). There is also "no truth in itself of the sexual difference in itself, of either man or woman in itself" (*SNS*, 103). All of ontology, however, "with its inspection, appropriation, identification and verification of identity," conceals this "undecidability" at the same time as it is presupposed (*SNS*, 105). In this regard the question of woman "suspends the decidable opposition of true and non-true" (*SNS*, 107). In the process "the epochal regime of quotation marks" is inaugurated, "which is to be enforced for every concept belonging to the system of philosophical decidability" (*SNS*, 107). "The hermeneutic project" now appears illegitimate, and in the process "reading is freed from the horizon of the meaning or truth of being, liberated from the values of the product's production or the present's presence" (*SNS*, 107). The effect is that "the question of style is immediately unloosed as a question of writing. The question posed by the spurring-operation (*opération-éperonnante*) is more powerful than any content, thesis or meaning" (*SNS*, 107).

Heidegger's reading of Nietzsche, by contrast, "missed the woman in truth's fabulous plot-ting," by not raising the sexual question or by subsuming "it in the general question of truth" (*SNS*, 109). For Derrida and for Nietzsche, however, these questions of regional or fundamental ontology can have no "authentic" answers, since they may no longer even be questions. According to Nietzsche's analysis of sexual difference, for example, there are no fixed or persisting orderings, there is only a "process of *propriation*" of constantly changing relations that escapes "not only dialectics, but also any ontological decidability" (*SNS*, 111). Derrida concentrates on one moment in this exchange, that of "giving oneself for": "The *for* which appears in the 'to-give-oneself-for,' whatever its value, whether it deceives by giving only an appearance of, or whether it actually introduces some destination, finality or twisted calculation, some return, redemption or gain, into the loss of proper-ty [*propre*], this *for* nevertheless continues to withhold the gift of a reserve. Henceforth all the signs of a sexual opposition are changed. Man and woman change places" (*SNS*, 111). Although he does not treat the topic explicitly in this text, Derrida detaches from Marxism and from dialectics in general his propriation theory of man and woman, mastery and servitude, appropriation and expropriation. Instead of a Marxist or dialectical order, however, his differential theory of signs appears again through the various levels of irony. The question of what these things are, "the question *ti esti*," becomes superfluous, since the propriation process "organized both the totality of language's process and symbolic exchange in general" (*SNS*, 111). Derrida summarizes:

The history (of) truth (is) a process of propriation. And it is not from an onto-phenomenological or semantico-hermeneutic interrogation that proper-ty [*propre*] is to be derived. For the question of the truth of being is not *capable* of the question of proper-ty [*propre*]. On the contrary, it falls short of the undecidable exchange of more into less. Already inscribed in the give-take, give-keep, give-jeopardize, in short in the *coup de don*, this question is incapable of answering for them.   (*SNS*, 111–13)

He concludes with the same point in different terms: "The question of proper-ty [*propre*] has only to loom up in the field of economy (in its restricted sense), linguistics, rhetoric, psychoanalysis, politics, etc., for the onto-hermeneutic interrogation to reveal its limit" (*SNS*, 113).

Although at this point neither "hard" nor "soft" readers of Nietzsche would be likely to think of Heidegger, Derrida nevertheless returns to and includes both Heidegger's onto-hermeneutic reading and his "delimitation of the ontological problematic" (*SNS*, 115). He finds the opening moment in "the enigmatic operation of the abyssal gift" (*SNS*, 121), to which

Heidegger had submitted the question of Being itself in his lecture "Time and Being" (1962) (*OTB*, 1–24). In this text there occurs a process of propriation that "can be construed neither in the boundaries of Being's horizon nor from the vantage point of its truth, its meaning" (*SNS*, 121). More important is the famous conclusion of the lecture, which appears under the heading: "I have forgotten my umbrella" (*SNS*, 123). The heading is a verbatim quotation of a fragment that appears in the fifth section of the Critical Complete Edition (*KSA*, 9: 587). In the closing section of his lecture, Derrida considers this fragment and addresses some of the hermeneutic questions provoked by such a text: "Maybe a citation. It might have been a sample picked up somewhere, or overheard here or there. Perhaps it was the note for some phrase to be written here or there" (*SNS*, 123). We may never know. The editors who annotated Nietzsche's *inedita* must have been led by a "hermeneutic somnambulism" when they said they would retain, for the selection and organization of the manuscripts, only those pieces related to the works he finished (*SNS*, 125).

In order to appreciate these sarcastic allusions we must recall that Derrida is referring here, among other things, to a "stormy encounter" he had with a hermeneut around 1967, about the time when the new Critical Edition was begun (*SNS*, 139). This person had tried to ridicule the publication of all of Nietzsche's unpublished manuscripts: "They will end up," he said, "publishing his laundry notes and scraps like 'I have forgotten my umbrella'" (*SNS*, 139).

Another point of connection to the umbrella can be found, as Derrida remarks, in Heidegger's *Question of Being* (*QB*). In this 1955 text, Heidegger assesses "the culminating phase of nihilism," in which "it seems that there is no such thing as the '*Being of being*,' that there is nothing to it" (*SNS*, 141). "Being remains absent in a singular way," reported Heidegger, who printed the word "Being" crossed through with a dark "x" in order to express his uncertainty in this matter more forcefully. Being "remains in a veiled concealment [*Verborgenheit*] which itself veils itself" (*SNS*, 141). It is a question here of experiencing "the essence of forgetting," "in the way the Greeks experienced it," namely, as "nothing negative. Inasmuch as it is a concealment, however, it is no doubt a protective concealment which safeguards the still Undisclosed" (*SNS*, 141). We usually represent forgetting falsely, Heidegger argues, in such a way that "forgetting easily assumes the appearance of a simple lacuna, a lack, uncertainty" (*SNS*, 141). We normally consider that "to forget, to be forgetful, is exclusively 'to omit'"; hence it is seen as merely "a human condition" (*SNS*, 141). In Heidegger's way of thinking, the "forgetting of Being" [*Seinsvergessenheit*] has been represented in many ways "as if Being (figuratively speaking) were the umbrella that some philosophy professor, in his distraction, left somewhere" (*SNS*, 143). But with this view we remain far removed from "determining the essence of forgetting," for it "belongs to the nature of Being ('*Sie gehört zur Sache des Seins*') and reigns as the destiny of its essence ('*als Geschick seines Wesens*')" (*SNS*, 143).

Against the background of this and other connections, the "umbrella" fragment reveals its potential for the hermeneut. As Derrida comments, it may initially appear rather simple and unimportant. Its "inaccessibility," to be sure, "is not necessarily one of some hidden secret" (*SNS*, 125). Its easy "readability" gives it the "appearance of a more than flat intelligibility" (*SNS*, 129). The apparently self-evident meaning of the text is further enhanced because it contains "a stratum of readability" that "could eventually be translated with no loss into any language which disposes of a certain material" (*SNS*, 129). "No fold, no reserve, appears to mark its transparent display" (*SNS*, 129). Nevertheless, we know nothing about this fragment, and this unknowing "would withdraw it from any assured horizon of a hermeneutic question" (*SNS*, 127). Of course, other, "much more elaborated operations" of meaning could be mentioned. One could propose, for example, "a 'psychoanalytic' decoding," in which we "know" or think we know what the symbol of the umbrella means: "Take, for example, the hermaphroditic spur [*éperon*] of a phallus which is modestly enfolded in its veils, an organ which is at once aggressive and apotropaic, threatening and/or threatened. One doesn't just happen onto an unwonted object of this sort in a sewing-up machine [*machine à recoudre*] on a castration table" (*SNS*, 129–31). For Freud, in fact, the umbrella went far beyond a "symbolic object" and became a "metaphor of a metapsychological concept" (*SNS*, 131). Furthermore, psychoanalysis recognizes not only the umbrella but also the forgetting of the object. Hence it could be hoped that the analyst "might yet aspire to a hermeneutic mastery of these remains" (*SNS*, 131). With this hope, however, the analyst would join "in principle the impulsive reader or hermeneut ontologist in their common belief that this unpublished piece is an aphorism of some significance. Assured that it must mean something, they look for it to come from the most intimate reaches of this author's thought" (*SNS*, 131). In reality this is what we do not know; hence the "remainder" that is the phrase "I have forgotten my umbrella" "is not caught up in any circular trajectory" (*SNS*, 131). It has "no proper itinerary which would lead from its beginning to its end and back again, nor does its movement admit of any center" (*SNS*, 131). Structurally speaking, it is "liberated from any living meaning," and there occurs "no end to its parodying play with meaning, grafted here and there, beyond any contextual body or finite code":

It is quite possible that that published piece, precisely because it is readable as a piece of writing, should remain forever secret. Its secret is rather the possibility that indeed it might have no secret, that it might only be pretending to be simulating some hidden truth within its folds. Its limit is not only stipulated by its structure but is in fact intimately con-fused with it. The hermeneut cannot but be provoked and disconcerted by its play.   (*SNS*, 133)

As one will have noticed, Derrida self-ironically constructs his own theory of the text on the basis of this unlikely and somewhat empty fragment from Nietzsche's unpublished writings. To illustrate the point, it is useful to recall Derrida's most compact statement on the nature of the text, which he gave as a motto to his interpretation of Plato: "A text is not a text unless it hides from the first comer, from the first glance, the law of its composition and the rules of its game. A text remains, moreover, forever imperceptible. Its law and its rules are not, however, harbored in the inaccessibility of a secret; it is simply that they can never be booked, in the present, into anything that could rigorously be called a perception" (*DS*, 63).[4] Plato's text can indeed be seen as the prototype of what Derrida calls "the dissimulation of the woven texture" (*DS*, 63). For if Plato has become the king of logocentrism, who condemns with a sun-filled voice the arts, play, rhetoric, writing, and myth, he does all this in a text constituted by art, play, rhetoric, staged writing, and mythical narratives.[5] With this, Plato and Nietzsche remarkably begin to resemble each other for Derrida, although not as for Heidegger on the basis of an historical or an overturned metaphysics but on the level of textuality.

Derrida's concept of the text does not imply that we must abandon from the outset the project of knowing what the text says; once again that would be the reaction of "the aestheticizing and obscurantist *hermeneuein*" (*SNS*, 133). On the contrary, in order to take into account this "structural limit" and the "remainder of the simulacrum" of the text, the "process of decoding" should be "carried to the furthest lengths possible" (*SNS*, 128). The reader should adopt that form of active interpretation introduced by Nietzsche or practice the expository, mise-en-scène type of writing exemplified by Derrida in his own texts. Nevertheless, "this limit is not of the sort that circumscribes a certain knowledge even as it proclaims a beyond,"

[4]From Jacques Derrida, "Plato's Pharmacy," in *DS*, 62–172.

[5]See esp. the last section of "Plato's Pharmacy," entitled "Play: From the Pharmakon to the Letter and from Blindness to the Supplement" (*DS*, 156–72).

for "the limit runs through and divides a scientific work, whose very condition, this limit, thus opens it up to itself" (*SNS*, 133).

In regard to Nietzsche's text, then, Derrida's hypothesis is: "If Nietzsche had indeed meant to say something, might it not be just that limit to the will to mean, which, much as a necessarily differential will to power, is forever divided; folded and manifolded?" (*SNS*, 133) Derrida argues that this hypothesis "cannot be denied," no matter how far "one might carry a conscientious interpretation" (*SNS*, 133). This amounts to saying "that there is no 'totality to Nietzsche's text,' not even a fragmentary or aphoristic one" (*SNS*, 135). Such a conclusion, Derrida writes, would "expose one, roofless and unprotected by a lightning rod as he is, to the thunder and lightning of an enormous clap of laughter" (*SNS*, 135).

The next occasion for a critical confrontation with Nietzsche arose for Derrida a few years later with a seminar on the philosopher at the University of Virginia in 1976, on the occasion of the bicentennial of the American Declaration of Independence.[6] Should the American Declaration of Independence from the Old World be seen in the context of Nietzsche's turn away from the old metaphysics? That is hard to say, although the text takes its point of departure from the Declaration as well as from the signatures at the end of the text. These signatures are not merely an "empirical and thus reducible incident," as might be imagined in a scientific publication, "whose value can be separated without difficulty from the name of its

[6]In fact, Derrida had delivered the same lecture a year earlier under the title "La vie et la mort" (Life and death), at the Ecole normale supérieure in Paris. He opened at the University of Virginia, however, with a preamble on the Declaration of Independence and the lecture has been published in this form. The lecture appeared first in German in a translation (*NO*) by Friedrich Kittler; this version is the basis for my comments. The French text appeared somewhat later: Jacques Derrida, *Otobiographies: L'Enseignement de Nietzsche et la politique du nom propre* (Paris: Galilée, 1984). See note 8 to this chapter for later versions of the text.

author, indeed must be separated in order to make the claim for objectivity" (*NO*, 65). Examples would be Euclid's *Geometry* or Einstein's papers on relativity. A declaration, however, which founds an institution, implies "that the signatory is under an obligation to it," although at the same time the institution, which in its history and tradition must free itself from the individuals who had created it, nevertheless "preserves the signature in itself" (*NO*, 65).

Derrida follows this problem of signatures and the proper name as it leads to Nietzsche. The question arises: What does it mean when a philosopher of Nietzsche's acumen has his name attached to his philosophy or his text so that it can no longer be separated and seems to converge with the text? Derrida puts the question this way:

> The name of Nietzsche for us in the West today is perhaps the name of the only one (in a way different from Kierkegaard, perhaps, and perhaps like Freud) who has treated philosophy and life, science and the philosophy of life, *with his own name and in his own name.* He is perhaps the only one who has brought his name—his names—and his biography into play. With almost all the risks that this entails: for "him," for "them," for his life, his names and their future, above all the political future of what he has signed. How could this be left out of the account when he is read? He is only read when this is taken into account.   (*NO*, 72)

The topic of the proper name and the signature forms a distinct constellation in Derrida's theory of the text or science of writing.[7] It is clear from this passage that Derrida is also addressing the political implications of Nietzsche's writings. These would apparently be excluded in the treatment of Nietzsche's "styles" if one overlooks the analysis of the question of woman and the processes of propriation. But the "politics of the proper name" is only the second part of the title, which begins with the surprising formulation "Nietzsche's Otobiography," a reference to the Greek word for ear (*to ous,*

---

[7] See Jacques Derrida, "Signature Event Context," in *MP*, 307–30.

ōtos). The formulation seems to indicate that it is not so much the self (*autos*) that produces its autobiography but the ear of the other that receives the text of the writer and affixes the signature to it. Derrida organized a colloquium on the topic in Montreal, and parts of this text were used. But the theme extended far beyond Nietzsche and dealt with, for example, numerous other transferences or auditory transpositions of the text, such as translation.[8] Autobiography becomes effective, or so this connection could be formulated, "not when it apparently takes place but later, when ears have managed to receive its message" (*NO*, 72). The signature takes place on the side of the receiver. This includes political tasks for Derrida, since "we are the ones to whom responsibility for the signature of the text of the other has been entrusted, the text we have inherited" (*NO*, 72). The signature is not a word or a name at the end of a text, but the multiple operation of the text as a whole, the text as a whole that has left something behind. This understanding of signatures and texts indicates the complexity of the question of political responsibility for Derrida.[9]

The Virginia text, "Nietzsche's Otobiography or the Politics of the Proper Name," could therefore be read in a decisively anti-Heideggerian direction, since it was after all Heidegger's ear that heard a certain name of Nietzsche as absolutely separate from his proper name and the history of his life. "Nietzsche," as Heidegger explained the title of his *Nietzsche* in the first sentence of his preface, "the name of the thinker stands as the title for the *matter* of his thinking" (*N*, 1: xv). Derrida's text

[8] *L'oreille de l'autre, otobiographies, transferts, traductions, textes et débats avec Jacques Derrida*, comp. Claude Levesque and Christie V. McDonald (Montreal: VLB, 1982). For an English translation, see Jacques Derrida, *The Ear of the Other: Otobiography, Transference, Translation*, trans. Christie V. McDonald (New York: Schocken, 1985).

[9] See "L'oreille de l'autre" and the debates published in this collection (cited in the previous note), as well as the essay by Derrida, "Like the Sound of the Sea Deep Within a Shell: Paul de Man's War" (cited in note 38 to Chapter 1).

does not address this issue, however, but concerns itself with the more direct problem of how Nietzsche's name became entangled with the "worst moments of our time" (*NO*, 73).

This is particularly the main issue in the second part ("The Otographic Sign of the State"), which starts with the "question of institutions and teaching institutions" and turns to Nietzsche's early text "On the Future of Our Educational Institutions" (1872) (*NO*, 82). Derrida emphasizes here that it is not a matter of "neutralizing or defusing those parts of Nietzsche that can be unsettling for a democratic pedagogy or a 'left' politics" (*NO*, 82). Still less is it a matter of dissimulating the parts of Nietzsche's text "that could have served the darker needs of National Socialism as a 'language'" (*NO*, 83). Derrida argues instead that we must ask further "why it is insufficient to say that 'Nietzsche did not think that,' 'did not want that,' or 'would certainly have gotten sick over that,' and that a fraudulent testimony or interpretive mystification has occurred" (*NO*, 85). Derrida continues:

It will be asked why and how such a thing was possible, what such a naive fraudulence means (it was not successful with every writer), why and how "the same" words and "the same" expressions, in case they are the same, are multiply applicable in various meanings and contexts that are supposedly different, supposedly even irreconcilable. It will be asked why the only educational institution, the only sign of an educational institution that could refer to Nietzsche's doctrine or teaching about teaching was Nazi.   (*NO*, 85)

It would, of course, be "crude and naive" if the word "Führer" were simply taken from Nietzsche's text, "with its Hitlerian resonance and the echoes given it by Nazi orchestration" (*NO*, 88). But it would be equally shortsighted and somnambulist to say "that Nietzsche had never wanted or thought that," since one only has to remember that the "Hitlerian Führer" also wanted to be "a master of thought," or simply to refer to "the example of Heidegger" (*NO*, 89). Despite all these considerations, even if one speaks of the perversion or reversal of Nietzsche's thought, there still remains "the possibility of a

distortion and mimetic perversion to be explained" (*NO*, 90).
Derrida insists that "there is nothing absolutely contingent in
the case," since "the only politics that *really* elevated him as one
of its highest and official banners was Nazi":

By this I do not mean that this "Nietzschean" politics is the only one
possible, nor that it corresponds to the best reading of this heritage,
nor even that those unconnected with it have read Nietzsche better.
No. The future of Nietzsche's text is not closed. But since, in the still
open contours of an epoch, the only politics called "Nietzschean"
were Nazi, this is necessarily significant and must be questioned as
to its entire significance.   (*NO*, 91)

   The point at stake is that it makes little sense to read Nietzsche and his politics from the perspective of Nazism, for it
is by no means clear "that we know how to think Nazism"
and, on the other hand, that Nietzsche's text is "not closed."
Formulated more sharply: we cannot dismiss the question
whether Nietzsche's "grand politics" already lie behind us or
are "just now coming toward us," that is, "on the other side of
an upheaval of which National Socialism and Fascism were
only episodes" (*NO*, 91). Derrida points in this instance to passages like the one on "dynamite" in *Ecce Homo*: "I am no man,
I am dynamite" (*GM*, 326). But he also reminds us that in
Nietzsche's "On the Future of Our Educational Institutions"
the state is "the great accused," and Hegel is "the thinker of the
state, a great proper name for this guilty one." In fact, Nietzsche articulates his critique in a manner that would let the
"Marxist analysis of this apparatus and even its organizational
concept of 'ideology'" be seen as "a new form of subservience
under the Hegelian state" (*NO*, 93). To determine the relations
between the Marxist critique and Nietzsche's more precisely,
however, the "Marxist concepts of the state and Nietzsche's
opposition to socialism and democracy" would have to be considered more closely (*NO*, 93).
   In regard to Nietzsche's text on educational institutions in
particular, Derrida finds that we have every reason to recog-

nize ourselves in this early, intricate text, as in the "full score of a piece of music," that is, "every man of us," as he expressly states, not including women, for "woman, if I have read correctly, nowhere appears. Neither to study nor to teach, at no point in the umbilical cord" (*NO*, 93). Derrida modifies this point: "That is, no woman, if I have read correctly, except for the mother. But this belongs to the system, the mother is the figure without figure and the face of a *figuress*. She makes a space for all figures by losing herself as an anonymous shape in the background of the scene. Everything—and life, first of all—returns to her, everything is directed toward her and determined for her. She survives under the condition that she will remain in the background" (*NO*, 97).

The phenomenon of the mother also governs the first part of the text ("The Logic of the Living"), which deals with Nietzsche's autobiography more directly—in any case with his "otobiography"—the text of *Ecce Homo* as Derrida reads it. It involves the biography of the philosopher not only in the traditional sense, "in that ornamental style and type to which great historians of philosophy give themselves," but also in the sense of "psychobiographies that pretend to do justice to the emergence of a system by empirical processes of a psychological or even psychoanalytic, historical, or sociological type" (*NO*, 71). For Derrida it is a question of that "margin between 'work' and 'life,' between system and the subject of the system," which is questioned neither by the textually immanent readings of philosophical systems ("structuralist or not") nor by "external, empirical-genetic readings." Derrida adds: "This margin—I call it *dynamis* because of its force, its power, its virtual and also its movable potency—is neither active nor passive, neither inside nor outside" (*NO*, 71).

What is to be understood by this realm? We can specify it more closely through consideration of a broader dimension Derrida often borrows from Freudian discourse, although here only its outlines can be sketched. Life, or what is called life ("the matter or the object of biology and biography"), does not "oppose something that stands for its opposite: death, the thanatological or the thanatographic" (*NO*, 71). On the contrary, life "has difficulty becoming the object of a science in the sense that philosophy and other sciences have always given this word, with the legitimate status of a scientific method" (*NO*, 71–72). Sciences in this sense can dominate their object "without delay and residue," but they are essentially "sciences of the inorganic, stated differently, of the dead" (*NO*, 72). The science of life must necessarily deal with "delays" and "residues," which is not necessary when dealing with the conventional dead scientific object. Thus the "margin" of which Derrida speaks occurs between two "bodies," the body of the text and the person of the author (*NO*, 72). In this sense he suggests that "Nietzsche should be read from the scene of *Ecce Homo*," the text in which Nietzsche "brings forth his body and his name," "even when he operates in masks or pseudonyms without proper names" (*NO*, 73). Masks or plural names belong to that "protection benefit" and "surplus value" in which we can see the "cunning of life" (*NO*, 73), for "life is dissimulation" (*NO*, 75).

Derrida refers to the preface Nietzsche added to *Ecce Homo*, "How One Becomes What One Is," on his forty-fifth birthday, shortly before the end of his conscious life, which begins by stating his intention "to say *who I am*" (*GM*, 217). That day seemed to Nietzsche to be a "perfect day," the high point of life, "when everything is ripening and not only the grape turns brown," a day on which "the eye of the sun" fell on his life and let him "be grateful" for his whole life (*GM*, 221). That day prompted him to a decision to "tell my life to myself" (*GM*, 221). The fact that he wants to narrate "to himself" is connected with his idea of life on one's "own credit"; to this he added that it was "perhaps a mere prejudice" that he had lived, for in his environment "one has neither heard nor even seen me" (*GM*, 217). He needed only to speak with "one of the 'educated' who come to the Upper Engadine for the summer" to convince himself that he did not live (*GM*, 217). For this reason he felt obliged to say: *"Hear me! For I am such and such a person. Above all, do not mistake me for someone else"* (*GM*, 217).

To be sure, this "self-presentation on display" may result from the "cunning of dissimulation," Derrida adds, and could deceive us "if we want to hear it as a mere presentation of his identity" (*NO*, 75). But that presupposes that we already know "how a self-presentation and an explanation of identity are done" (*NO*, 75). That Nietzsche, however, mentions all this in a preface to the book *Ecce Homo* signed by Friedrich Nietzsche, a book whose last words are "Have I been understood?—*Dionysus versus the Crucified*" (*GM*, 335); that Nietzsche, furthermore, "as Ecce homo, or Christ, is not Christ, not even Dionysos, rather the name of the 'versus,' the antiname, the battle that announces and names itself between the two names"—all this seems for Derrida sufficient "to pluralize in a distinctive way the proper name and the homonymous mask and to entangle all the threads of the name in a labyrinth—the labyrinth of the ear, of course" (*NO*, 76).

Whereas in *Spurs* Derrida had emphasized Nietzsche's styles and the heterogeneity of Nietzsche's text, in his later writings Nietzsche's unique "double nature," his character as a "Doppelgänger," his signature, his life, and his biographical story reveal a "contradictory duplicity." Derrida sees this quality equally in the thought of the "midday of life," which is in fact "no place, no site," but an "immediately disappearing border," one that immediately eludes the thought of singularity when an attempt is made to grasp it. For Derrida, these reflections yield "an impossible program for reading and teaching, something of ridiculous absurdity, but also something dark, something of a dark and mischievous shadow history in the explanation that Friedrich Nietzsche said this or that, thought this or that, about life for example, in the sense of human existence or in the biological sense" (*NO*, 79). All statements, Derrida continues, "before and afterwards, left and right, are simultaneously possible (Nietzsche has more or less said everything) and necessarily contradictory (he has said things most irreconcilable with each other, and said that he was saying them)" (*NO*, 79).

Nietzsche himself highlights the "principle of contradiction" in his life, the "doubled truth" of his existence, as he indicates in the first chapter of *Ecce Homo*, "Why I Am So Wise" (*GM*, 222). Here he thematizes his "dual descent" and states at the outset: "The good fortune of my existence, its uniqueness perhaps, lies in its fatality: I am, to express it in the form of a riddle, already dead as my father, while as my mother I am still living and becoming old" (*GM*, 222). From this remark Derrida derives the principle of contradiction in Nietzsche's life, his existence "between the principle of death and the principle of life, end and beginning, depth and height, falling and rising, etc." (*NO*, 79). The father is the principle of death, the mother is that of "life, which persists, the living, those who are living" (*NO*, 79), and this to such an extent that she survives him, in any case in relation to Nietzsche's mental collapse. Derrida interprets this relation—"the dead or rather absent father and the mother who lives above all and after all"—as the "elementary structure of the relationship." "She had found her examples in great families, in the Pietà of the family of Jesus (which stands in opposition to Dionysos, but also as his mirrored 'Doppelgänger') and of Nietzsche, if it is remembered that the mother had survived the 'collapse'; and in general in all families, if one only 'pushes all facts aside'" (*NO*, 81).

Nietzsche himself saw the consequences of his "dual descent" from death and life, father and mother, in relation "to the total problem of life" and in the sense of "neutrality" and "freedom from all partiality," combining both rise and fall: "I know both, I am both" (*GM*, 222). This doubled series of experiences unites for him "the perfect brightness and cheerfulness, even exuberance of the spirit," with the "most profound physiological weakness," "even with an excess of pain" (*GM*, 222). These pains are described in some detail: "In the midst of the torments that go with an uninterrupted three-day migraine, accompanied by laborious vomiting of phlegm, I possessed a dialectician's clarity *par excellence* and thought through with very cold blood matters for which under healthier circumstances I am not mountain-climber, not subtle, not *cold* enough" (*GM*, 222–23). Nietzsche took his growing sense of a perspectivist optics as the most important consequence of his double nature. This was the "true gift" of those days of sickness "in which everything in me became subtler— observation itself as well as all organs of observation" (*GM*, 223).

He developed a notion of perspectivism explicitly through the concepts of sickness and health: "Looking from the perspective of the sick toward *healthier* concepts and values and, conversely, looking again from the fullness and self-assurance of a *rich* life down into the secret work of the instinct of decadence—in this I have had the longest training, my truest experience; if in anything, I became master in *this*. Now I know how, have the know-how, to *reverse perspectives*: the first reason why a revaluation of values is perhaps possible for me alone" (*GM*, 223). For Derrida, however, this "contradiction of the 'Doppelgänger'" goes beyond "what a merely dialectical opposition could contain of dissenting negativity" (*NO*, 82).

Derrida's third text on Nietzsche was given in April 1981 at the Goethe Institute in Paris, where he met with Hans-Georg Gadamer for a public philosophical dialogue with other German and French critics on the topic "text and interpretation." In the general reception of this debate, however, interest has concentrated on the exchange between the representative of philosophical hermeneutics and the proponent of deconstruction.[10] The discussion between Gadamer and Derrida occurred in several phases. In his introductory lecture on the topic "text and interpretation" (*DD*, 21–51), Gadamer not only set out the principles of his philosophical hermeneutics but in general

---

[10]The papers presented at this conference have appeared in German (*TUI*). For an English translation that includes several other essays by different critics, see *DD*.

characterized his motivation as the "good will to understanding," in order to build a bridge for discussion with Derrida.
Derrida answered, however, with a statement entitled somewhat dismissively as "Good Will to Power," perhaps in order
to suggest how much of a will to domination, appropriation,
classification, reduction, and castration operates within the
"good will to understanding" claimed by hermeneutics (*DD*,
52–54). He basically addressed three critical questions to Gadamer about the "universality claim" of hermeneutics, questions
that try to indicate "a quite different way of thinking about
texts" than the one offered by Gadamer (*DD*, 54).[11]

The turn to Nietzsche intensified in this debate when Gadamer, in his reply entitled "And Nevertheless: The Power of
Good Will," tried to locate Derrida's statements within the
principles and universality claim of hermeneutics. At this point
Derrida sharply disrupted the frame of the debate; he gave his
answer the title "Interpreting Signatures (Nietzsche/Heideg-
ger): Two Questions" and, in place of a direct answer to Gadamer's "good-will effort," replied with a critical-philological
analysis of Heidegger's *Nietzsche* (*DD*, 58–71). It is evident,
however, that Derrida was operating paradigmatically in taking Heidegger's *Nietzsche* as the most blatant example of how
philosophical hermeneutics, from Derrida's perspective, proceeds. Gadamer could not have been unhappy with this, since
he himself at many times and even on the previous evening of
the debate had designated Heidegger's *Nietzsche* as a masterpiece of philosophical interpretation, in which Heidegger had
succeeded in reaching the decisive insight that the will to
power and the eternal recurrence of the same belong together
and "are only two aspects of the same thing."[12]

Derrida's text on Nietzsche, then, can be read as part of the

[11] See Chapter 5 for a discussion of this issue.

[12] See Hans-Georg Gadamer, "Das Drama Zarathustras," *Nietzsche-
Studien* 15 (1986): 3–4; and the interview of Gadamer by Philippe Forget
and Jacques Le Rider: "Hans-Georg Gadamer et le pouvoir de la philosophie," *Le Monde*, Apr. 18/19, 1981.

"German-French debate" staged at the 1981 conference and can be understood without bringing the multiple perspectives and pluralistic forms of his image of Nietzsche into play. As the title "Interpreting Signatures" announces, however, this text continues the argument developed in the "otobiography" through an autobiographical interpretation and beyond. The text also enters into a broader confrontation with Heidegger's image of Nietzsche, which has been important for Derrida's work on Nietzsche from the outset.

Two features expand Derrida's analysis of Nietzsche considerably. Once again, however, Derrida's studies of Nietzsche do not present a complete, finished vision but deliberately retain the character of a fragmentary, perspectival set of notes or occasional comments about Nietzsche that might well lead to new deliberations. Accordingly, Derrida concludes the essay with the remark that he has managed only to sketch "two questions" and that he will "perhaps" return to the "metonymical violence" which governs the interpretation of Nietzsche "somewhere else, some other time" (*DD*, 71).

Derrida's text does in fact address two questions: the first "concerns the *name* Nietzsche," and the second "has to do with the concept of totality" (*DD*, 58). Yet the first question dominates the text in general, which primarily presents Derrida's most fundamental confrontation with Heidegger's image of Nietzsche. Wherever one opens Heidegger's text, in the lectures on the eternal recurrence of the same or those on the will to power as knowledge, Derrida sees "that the same interpretation is regularly at work throughout" and that a "single system of reading is powerfully concentrated and gathered together" (*DD*, 58). Insistently, the interpretation addresses "the unity and the uniqueness of Nietzsche's thinking" (*DD*, 58). This thinking is interpreted "as a fulfilled unity" and seems for Heidegger to reach "the culmination of Western metaphysics," to be in a sense "the crest, or ridge, atop the peak of this fulfillment" (*DD*, 58). If, however, one looks behind this "reading of Nietzsche," one sees "the foundations of a general reading of Western metaphysics" (*DD*, 59). The question then arises of how "this interpretation in its totality and as a whole" in relation to Nietzsche can include "an interpretive decision about the unity or singularity of thinking" (*DD*, 59). For Heidegger, the decision regarding the unity of Nietzsche's philosophy does not derive from Nietzsche himself. It is not constituted "by the life of Nietzsche, either normal or insane," but results instead "from the unity of Western metaphysics," so that "biography, autobiography, the scene or the powers of the proper name, of proper names, signatures, and so on, are again accorded minority status, are again given the inessential place they have always occupied in the history of metaphysics" (*DD*, 59). This means, however, as Derrida remarks, that "the unity of his interpretation of Nietzsche, the unity of Western metaphysics to which this interpretation is referred, and the unity of the Heideggerian path of thought are here inseparable. One cannot think the one without the other" (*DD*, 59–60).

Derrida begins his analysis with "a provisional concession to the classical norms of reading" by undertaking a minute analysis of Heidegger's text, but he runs into complications with the first sentence of the preface (" 'Nietzsche'—the name of the thinker stands as the title for the *matter* of his thinking"; *N*, 1: xv). The question arises: "Now, what happens when a proper name is put between quotation marks?" (*DD*, 60). The "*Sache*" (matter), as Heidegger says, does not stand here for the "cause," but for the "quarrel" that is "confrontation in itself," the Latin "*causa*," or "legal debate." It is thus not the case that the "name" Nietzsche determines his thinking in the same way as the cause of a material effect. The syntax shows, rather, that the genitive must be read in the other direction: the name is not prior to the thought but is the "subject-matter" of the thought; " 'Nietzsche' is nothing other than the name of this thinking" (*DD*, 61). Derrida takes here a Heideggerian position, similar to the one Heidegger indicated later in the first volume of his *Nietzsche*: "*Who Nietzsche is* and what his name says can only authentically be experienced from his thinking,

not from a more or less refined biographical card catalogue"
(*DD*, 61).

The interpretation of Nietzsche from the name and the
name from the thinking can be articulated in two fundamentally different directions. One would consist in researching the
problematic of the name in a new way, "at the risk of seeing
the name dismembered and multiplied in masks and simula-
crae" (*DD*, 62). In this perspective one must take into account
that the name is never complete, for it "would be constituted
on the far side of the 'life' of the thinker," namely, "from the
vantage point of the future of the world" (*DD*, 62). This is the
path taken by Derrida in his "otobiography" of Nietzsche.
The other path would be to try "to determine the essentiality
of the name from the 'subject matter of thought,'" in fact from
a kind of thinking that has been explicated "as the content of
theses" (*DD*, 62). In this perspective "the particular proper
name" would "fall into inessentiality," into the "index of the
'biography' or a 'psychology' of an individual" (*DD*, 62). This
is the path followed by Heidegger. With a "gesture from classical metaphysics," he separates life and thought and detaches
from a summarily reported biography the "great questions"
Nietzsche had debated throughout his life.

The philological-historical basis of this hermeneutics appears in Heidegger's biting critique of the edition of the *Complete Works* published in the early twentieth century,[13] as well
as the historical-critical *Complete Works* from the Nazi period.[14] According to Heidegger, these editions rest on a false
"principle of completeness," according to which one must publish "absolutely everything" ("I have forgotten my umbrella")
and, in the "manner of biographical-psychological commentary," verify all dates in the life of the subject and even the

[13] Friedrich Nietzsche, *Sämtliche Werke*, Grossoktavausgabe (Leipzig:
Naumann, 1901–13).

[14] Friedrich Nietzsche, *Werke und Briefe*, Historisch-Kritische Gesamtausgabe (Munich: Beck, 1933–42).

comments of his contemporaries (*N*, 1: 10–11). The "compilation of the authentic 'work' (1881–1889)," dealing with the period of unpublished fragments from which *The Will to Power* was compiled, was for Heidegger a "task for the future" (*N*, 1: 11). It is evident from such comments that Heidegger envisioned a revised, new edition of this falsification, organized more strictly according to the principles of his interpretation of Nietzsche.

A further condition for Heidegger's Nietzsche, as Derrida demonstrates in his critique, consists in the claim that we will never be able to achieve an "authentic" interpretation of Nietzsche "if in the questioning we do not grasp Nietzsche as the end of Western metaphysics and press over to the quite different question of the truth of Being" (*N*, 1: 10). Derrida argues that "prior to all other questions, we need to be attentive to the fundamental necessity for such a schema as Heidegger puts forward" (*DD*, 63). In the course of actual interpretation, one should constantly situate Nietzsche within Western metaphysics and exile the question of truth to the other side of ontology. Only then, according to Heidegger, can we know "who Nietzsche was" (*DD*, 63).

The critique of this particular type of name interpretation is the first point in Derrida's confrontation with Heidegger's *Nietzsche*. In order to protect himself against simplifications, and with a characteristic gesture of acknowledgment to Heidegger's philosophical treatise, Derrida adds that Heidegger's method of interpreting Nietzsche, based on "the question 'Who is X?,'" was at the time "a rare question when applied to a thinker" and remains a rarity today. All too often this question is raised "in a biographically trivial way—as the man and the work, the man behind the work, the life of Descartes or Hegel associated with a kind of doxography" (*DD*, 64). That other way of interpreting Nietzsche, however, the path taken by Heidegger, to ask who Nietzsche was by making "his name the title of a book on his thought," is for Derrida highly unconventional (*DD*, 64). The topics of the "signature," the proper

name, the otobiography and autobiography, all of great importance for Derrida's theory of the text, form the starting point
for his critique of Heidegger's *Nietzsche* and to a certain extent
derive from Heidegger's impulse. To be sure, Derrida's own
styles shape his particular type of interpretation in such a way
that a decisive break with Heidegger occurs. To characterize
this breaking point or the separation from Heidegger more
precisely, Heidegger relates Nietzsche's name to a past or
closed event, a definable, coordinated, and concluded moment,
whereas Derrida situates the name in relation to an unforesee-
able, open-ended future.

The other important point in Derrida's critique of Heidegger's interpretation of Nietzsche is Heidegger's consistent intention "to rescue Nietzsche from his own singular fate" (*DD*,
65). Nietzsche's fate "remained ambiguous" for Heidegger, because his thinking had not found complete expression in his
writings and his interpreters had misunderstood him as writing a philosophy of life or poetic philosophy. Heidegger was
therefore concerned to gain access "to this innermost will and
to oppose it to the duplicity of the empirical figure of Nietzsche
as well as to the ambiguity of its subsequent effects" (*DD*, 65).
In the process he engaged in a problematic rescue mission,
since Nietzsche's thinking had not really "gone beyond the end
of metaphysics," according to Heidegger, but had remained
embedded in it (*DD*, 65). Derrida uncovers the duplicity of this
move: "In saving Nietzsche, Heidegger loses him too; he wants
at the same time to save him and let go of him. At the very
moment of affirming the uniqueness of Nietzsche's thinking,
he does everything he can to show that it repeats the mightiest
(and therefore the most general) schema of metaphysics" (*DD*,
65). This "ambiguous life-saving act" resembles one in which
the net is stretched out "for the tightrope walker, the one who
runs the greatest risk overhead on the narrow rope, only insofar as one has made sure that he—unmasked and protected by
the unity of his name, which in turn will be sealed by the unity

of metaphysics—will not be taking any risks. In other words: he was dead before he landed in the net" (*DD*, 69).

With an apparently trivial example, Derrida captures the basic procedures of Heidegger's reading of Nietzsche. The example concerns the epigraph of Heidegger's *Nietzsche*, which is taken from the aphorism entitled "In media vita" from *The Gay Science* (*GS*, 255). Heidegger cites this text only partially, making a number of important omissions that reduce the complex, multiply formed, difficult text to a one-dimensional line of thought; moreover, he introduces it with the comment: "Nietzsche himself names the experience that determines his thinking" (*DD*, 67). If the two texts are set next to each other, one has a powerful example of how the Heideggerian *Nietzsche* relates to Nietzsche. Derrida describes this relation:

And yet the paradoxical character of this passage (*In media vita!*) could also thwart Heidegger's hermeneutical strategy. Life does have a beyond, but it does not allow itself to be made into something secondary. As itself and in itself it unfolds the movement of truth or knowledge. It is in itself as its own beyond. Not to mention the stresses and the joys, the laughter and the war, the question marks and exclamation points—those things that Heidegger, considering how he effaces or conceals them, obviously does not want to hear spoken of here.   (*DD*, 66–67)

Such concealment typifies for Derrida the confrontations between "the Nietzsches and Martin Heidegger, between the Nietzsches and so-called [*ladite*] Western metaphysics" (*DD*, 68). He further describes this opposition: "Since Aristotle, and at least up until Bergson, 'it' [*metaphysics*] has constantly repeated and assumed that to think and to say must mean to think and say something that would be a *one*, one *matter*. And that not thinking-saying some one matter or principle is not thinking-saying at all, but a loss of the *logos*. Here is perhaps what the Nietzsches have put in question: the *legein* of this *logos*, the *gathering* of this logic" (*DD*, 68). The plurality in this name ("the Nietzsches") is for Derrida "like the family names of wanderers and tightrope walkers" and has led him to a "feast" (*DD*, 68). Heidegger also returns to the motif of the feast, which had been frequently used by Nietzsche, but interprets it in such a way that Nietzsche "can think of it only on the basis of his fundamental conception of all being, will to power." Heidegger sees in the reflection on this thought the festive character of his own lectures on Nietzsche (*N*, 1: 5–6). For Derrida, by contrast, the thinker at "the Nietzsches' feast" runs the "risk" of being torn to pieces and having his or her masks dispersed. He argues that the scene for Heidegger's feast was set not at Zarathustra's, "nor in Basel, Venice, or Nice [places Nietzsche lived]—but in Freiburg im Breisgau [Heidegger's home], between 1936 and 1940, during the preparation for a feast, preparation for a being 'at home in genuine questioning'" (*DD*, 68).

5

Deconstruction Versus Hermeneutics

"Interpreting Signatures (Nietzsche/Heidegger)" is Derrida's answer to the challenge of philosophical hermeneutics and his contribution to the "German-French debate" in philosophy. To understand his position fully, however, this text must be seen in a context not of Derrida's reading of Nietzsche but of his intensive engagement with German philosophy, particularly Hegel, Husserl, and Heidegger. From this perspective, his position on philosophical hermeneutics gains its characteristic profile.

Husserl and transcendental phenomenology are of decisive importance in this context, for they have determined Derrida's intellectual orientation at least as much as Saussure and the new linguistics and semiotics. Hence it would be incorrect to view the debate between Gadamer and Derrida as a dispute between two followers of Heidegger. Derrida has often remarked regarding his relation to German philosophy that his starting point precedes Heidegger and derives from transcendental phenomenology. In one instance, for example, he characterizes his philosophical path as a "perhaps endless passage through Husserl's transcendental phenomenology," as a "kind of fidelity" to this philosophy, which "makes certain demands of itself with the greatest rigor, even after one has deconstructed, as I have tried to do, a kind of fundamental level and in particular its intuitionist, pre-linguistic, or pre-semiotic axioms." [1] At another point Derrida describes transcendental phenomenology as a "discipline of incomparable rigor," which represents metaphysics in its most wakeful, most vigilant form (*TT*, 38). I will analyze this background for its most important features, before situating Derrida's interpretation of Nietzsche in the contemporary debate.

Derrida's relation to Husserl appears most prominently in the project of a theory of writing, which Derrida announces in terms of the question of the "ideality of the literary object" in the realm of Husserl's "ideal" objects. In Derrida's own words, he is concerned with the problem "What is literature? And first of all what is it to write? And even what does it mean?" He continues with a description of his philosophical beginnings: "To say this in other words—and here is the *saying otherwise* that was of importance to me—when and how does an inscription become literature and what takes place when it does? To what and to whom is it due? What takes place between philosophy and literature, science and literature, politics and literature, theology and literature, psychoanalysis and literature? It was here, in all the abstractness of its title, that lay the most pressing question" (*TT*, 37–38).

Derrida is referring here to his early writing on Husserl's *The Origin of Geometry* [2] and its exploration of the question: Under what circumstances do ideal objects become spatial and temporal when they enter history, that is, when they are written down? [3] At issue is the central question in Husserl's thought, which, although pursued by Husserl entirely in the sense of transcendental phenomenology, introduced prob-

[1] Jacques Derrida, "Antwort an Apel," *Zeitmitschrift: Journal für Aesthetik* 3 (Summer 1987): 76–84.

[2] See *Husserliana* 4 (1954): 365–86. For more accessible versions, see the following note. Citations of *OG* refer to the pages of the original edition, which is reproduced in Derrida's translation as well as in the German edition of Derrida's text.

[3] See *OG*. The introduction to this relatively short text forms the bulk of the edition, which has also appeared in German (cited as *HW*).

lems—such as the necessity of language itself—into the debate that could not be solved by the methods of transcendental phenomenology. As Derrida expresses it, Husserl did not notice the "threat that the logic of this inscription posed for the phenomenological project itself" (*TT*, 39). By contrast, Derrida concentrates on what he calls the "un-thought out axiomatics of Husserlian phenomenology," namely, its "'principle of principles,' that is to say, its intuitionism, the absolute privilege of the living present, the lack of attention paid to the problem of its own phenomenological enunciation, to transcendental discourse itself" (*TT*, 39). Husserl had envisioned, in *The Origin of Geometry*, the embodiment of the ideal object in writing as its ideal formation.[4] Only through the written, documenting, linguistic expression that can be reactivated again and again do ideal objects attain for Husserl an "enduring existence," their "unceasing being," which they cannot achieve in oral communication. An ideal structure like geometry "sediments" itself in the writing and "has become virtual communication" (*OG*, 371).

In Derrida's terms, writing, script, *écriture*, guarantee for Husserl the "absolute ability of the object to be transmitted, its absolutely ideal objectivity, and thus the purity of its relation to a universal transcendental subjectivity" (*HW*, 116). Of course, oral speech frees the object from a merely individual existence, but the object remains bound to its "synchronic exchange within the *community of authors*," within the "original, founding geometer" (*HW*, 116). Only through script does it become "free from every bond to an actual subjectivity" (*HW*, 116). To be sure, Husserl held to the metaphysical priority of the voice over script; his entire theory of the "living present" drove him to that decision. Written production or sedimentation was for him only a means for the ever-possible translation

[4]See Rudolf Bernet, "Differenz und Abwesenheit: Derrida und Husserls Phänomenologie der Sprache, der Zeit, der Geschichte, der wissenschaftlichen Rationalität," in *Studien zur neueren französischen Phänomenologie: Phänomenologische Forschungen* 18 (1986): 83–99.

back into voice, its "reactivation." Nevertheless, he attached
enormous significance to writing and said that through written
signs "the integration of human beings into a community will
be raised to a new level" (*OG*, 371). Husserl, in fact, gave literature a privileged position in the necessarily sensory embodiment of ideal objects, insofar as it, in its widest sense as
writing, circumscribes "all" the ideal objects of the sciences,
mathematics, philosophy, and the "products of belle-lettres."
The "objective being" of ideal objects consists in "being lin-
guistically expressed and repeatedly expressible, more distinct,
only having objectivity and existence for everyone as significance, the sense of speech" (*OG*, 208).

Language and "linguistic materiality" became for Husserl
of primary importance for "the functioning of human beings in humanity and the world as the horizon of human
existence" (*OG*, 369). Consciously alive in the world, we
become aware of it "as the horizon of our life," and in this
"world horizon" the "horizon of our fellow humans" is particularly "privileged" (*OG*, 369). We are always conscious of
our "shared humanity," our acquaintances, next of kin, or others, "for I can enter into an actual and potential, immediate
and mediated, empathic connection with them, a mutual understanding with others, and on the basis of this connection, I
can communicate with them, enter into a community with
them in various ways and then, regularly, learn from this com-
munal situation" (*OG*, 369). In this "horizon of humanity," the
"universal language" is fundamental: "Humanity is conscious
from the beginning as an immediate and mediated language
community" (*OG*, 369).

Of particular importance here is Husserl's concept of signs,
for his sign theory has little to do with language, text, and
interpretation in our contemporary use of these words. His
theory views language primarily from a logical and epistemological perspective and treats grammar principally as logical.
Moreover, Husserl's sign theory assumes a complete congruence between expression and meaning. Expression, as Husserl

states in the first of his *Logical Investigations*, is not the sign of something (symptom or marking) but has an ideal meaning that excludes polysemy.[5] The "we-horizon" of humanity is "a community based on the ability to articulate normally in a complete and mutually understandable way." Within this horizon "everyone could describe everything that is in the environment of humanity as objectively existing." The "objective world is from the outset the world for all who have 'everyman' as a world horizon" (*OG*, 370). Consequently Husserl saw in the turning to the "ways of apperception of a time-bound humanity" a mere romanticism, an interest in "pre-history" and "mythical-magical" experiences. In these evasions Husserl overlooked the "actual problem" and did not see that all "facticities" have a "root in the essential condition of universal humanity, in which the teleological reason moving through all historicity becomes evident." One problem he considered at this point referred to "the totality of history and the total meaning that finally gives it unity" (*OG*, 386).

For Derrida, by contrast, all signs demand an interpretation since they stand in a spatiotemporal context and possess attributes creating differences between them and what they signify. The "virtuality" of writing is deeply ambivalent for him. On the one hand it constitutes a grounding, but on the other hand, through passivity, forgetting, and the death of all phenomena, it produces a crisis (*HW*, 117). Derrida refers to the "silence of prehistoric culture and sunken civilizations, the buried condition of lost intentions and protected secrets, the illegibility of stone inscriptions" (*HW*, 118). All these phenomena betray the "transcendental sense of death," namely, the unity of death "with the absoluteness of intentional justice in the moment of its breakdown" (*HW*, 118).

Derrida's critique of Husserl's sign theory begins precisely at this point. He concentrates on the central principle of

[5]Edmund Husserl, *Logische Untersuchungen*, facsimile reproduction of the last edition (Tübingen: Niemeyer, 1980), 2: 1, 23–60.

transcendental phenomenology, which has always been the "ether" of metaphysics: the non-spatial and atemporal self-presentation of meaning and sense in a "living self-present," or in consciousness. As Derrida previously indicated in "La Différance," his effort in the critique of Husserl is to demonstrate that this supposed presence and self-presence in consciousness is not a priori but derivative, an effect, a determination resulting from the play of differences (*MP*, 1–27). In his text on Husserl's sign theory, the concept of the living self-presence of consciousness dissolves through the figurative character of language, the "stream of consciousness," "inner consciousness of time," the "lifeworld," the constant approximation of a final goal and all relations to a non-presence enclosed within these experiences: non-identity inscribed in the present as well as death inscribed in life (*SP*, 17–26).

Of course, the concept of a transcendental consciousness independent from language, time, and the lifeworld also became problematic for Husserl. As Derrida stated in his analysis of Husserl's *The Origin of Geometry*, his reading and deconstruction of Husserl's "pre-semiotic axioms" derived in fact from Husserl's text and arose from the instability of Husserl's principles. Presentation becomes the representation of representation, as in those sixteenth- and seventeenth-century Flemish genre paintings referred to by Husserl himself, for example, those by David Teniers in the Dresden Galerie, which through the depiction of images in mirrors give the impression of an infinite mirroring. Husserl, who became confused by such mirroring, wanted, in "the broad daylight of presence, outside the gallery," to grasp and to understand, or rather to comprehend, these infinite referrals and substitutions by intuitions and presentations (*SP*, 104). But as Derrida replied: "Certainly nothing has preceded this situation. Assuredly nothing will suspend it" (*SP*, 104).

These observations summarize Derrida's reading of Husserl. For the topic of the German-French debate and the dispute with philosophical hermeneutics, it is significant that

Derrida's intellectual starting point in philosophical-historical terms is Husserl and not Heidegger and that from the beginning he has concentrated on a sign theory. Of course, Derrida, like Heidegger, posits the finite, contextualized self marked by death in opposition to the transcendental self of phenomenology. But for Derrida this position results not from an existential analysis carried out in a crisis situation, as it had for the generation of World War I, but from his theory of the sign, of writing, of difference, the de-centered structure, substitutionality, infinite referrals, and active interpretation, in which Nietzsche, Freud, Heidegger, and Saussure all played active roles. The affinity to Heidegger seems therefore to occur primarily in regard to the late Heidegger of the critique of metaphysics and the self-critique of philosophy, Heidegger after World War II: the writer who, in other words, emerged with the *Letter on Humanism*, after ten years of studying Nietzsche.

Seen from this perspective, however, hermeneutics—if it were to be classified in terms of the history of philosophy, the history of metaphysics, and the history of Being—would be situated before the late Heidegger. Hermeneutics would be located in the phase of the phenomenological, transcendental analysis of Dasein that Heidegger left behind, since phenomenology, transcendentalism, and hermeneutics also belong to the history of ontology and are thus not in the position to suspend it.[6] To classify hermeneutics in this way is useful for understanding Derrida's view of it in the course of the German-French debate—not in order to dismiss hermeneutics as an out-of-date style of thought still embedded in metaphysics, a

[6]See Ernst Behler, "Deconstruction Versus Hermeneutics: Derrida and Gadamer on Text and Interpretation," *Southern Humanities Review* 21 (1987): 201–23. On Heidegger's connection to hermeneutic philosophy, see Otto Pöggeler, *Heidegger und die hermeneutische Philosophie* (Munich: Alber, 1983), as well as the anthology *Hermeneutische Philosophie*, ed. Otto Pöggeler (Munich: Nymphenburger Verlagshandlung, 1972), and esp. Hans-Georg Gadamer, *Truth and Method*, trans. Garrett Barden and John Cumming (New York: Seabury Press, 1975).

style no longer worth reading, but in order to assess more accurately the incommensurability and incompatibility of the two positions. Derrida's first question to Gadamer after his lecture, not coincidentally, was whether the formulation of a "good will to understanding" did not belong, "in its very necessity," "to a past epoch, namely, that of a metaphysics of the will?" (*DD*, 53)

The point can be sharpened. In his address, Gadamer had offered the "good will to understanding" with as much readiness, generosity, and eloquence as possible in order to establish a shared basis for conversation. Derrida parried this with the exclamation: "How could anyone not be tempted to acknowledge how extremely evident this axiom is?" (*DD*, 52) Clearly Derrida was aware that an endorsement of this axiom would entrap him in hermeneutic discourse, with all of its metaphysical implications. Subsequently Gadamer answered the few unconnected remarks made by Derrida with the heavy weapons of hermeneutics, particularly the claim to universality: "Whoever opens his mouth wants to be understood; otherwise, one would neither speak nor write" (*DD*, 55). In this way Gadamer prescribed the conditions of the discourse for Derrida; the offered understanding would take place in one direction only. In order to circumvent this hermeneutic "order of the discourse," Derrida could do little more than to formulate a few oblique questions. He thereby sought to bring forward a way of thinking about texts "quite different" from the one typically endorsed by hermeneutics (*DD*, 54). At the same time, in his original title he gently denounced the hermeneutic will to understanding as the "good will to power" (*DD*, 52).

In particular, Derrida inquired further into the "axiomatic precondition of interpretive discourse" suggested by Gadamer with his notions of "'*Verstehen*,' 'understanding the other,' and 'understanding one another'" (*DD*, 53). He began by asking: Is it a necessary given, for example, that the "precondition for Verstehen" is a continuously expanding relation, testifying to the "continuity of *rapport*," or is the model "not rather the interruption of *rapport*, a certain *rapport* of interruption, the suspending of all mediation?" (*DD*, 53) In other words, Derrida was not at all certain whether the experience underlying Gadamer's hermeneutics in general can in fact be generalized; whether, in fact, it was possible to know "in a dialogue that one has been perfectly understood" or to experience "the self-congratulatory success of confirmation" (*DD*, 54). This was, however, his third and last question.

Derrida's second question drew attention to the problem of relation, coherence, and "the living experience of living dialogue" and problematized this theme from the perspective of psychoanalysis, which, according to Derrida, equally undermines hermeneutics' claim to universality. Concepts such as "lived experience" and "context-related coherence" become problematic; at any rate the possibility arises that "not every coherence necessarily takes systematic form" (*DD*, 53). How should we define context, the "enlargement of a context"? (*DD*, 53) Should it be understood as "a continual expansion," in the style of hermeneutics, or as "a discontinuous restructuring," as it is seen in deconstruction? (*DD*, 53)

These remarks raise several fundamental and critical issues for hermeneutics and lead to the difficult problem of how Derrida's critique of hermeneutics is to be understood.[7] Does it involve a general dismissal of the process of understanding, or does it suggest another model of understanding, a deconstructive hermeneutics? Might this "other model" abstain from the gathering, propriative tendencies of hermeneutic understanding, with its inclination to reduce the object of cognition to serve its own purposes, yet conceive of itself as a specific type of interpretation, a kind of "active interpretation"? The question would then arise of whether Derrida's view of hermeneutics is correct in the first place. The time is long since past when

---

[7]Several responses to and essays on this debate are included in the second and third parts of *DD*.

hermeneutics was conceived as a procedure devoted to canonical understanding, authorial intention, and interpretation,
concentrating on the equation of expression with meaning;
now it proceeds according to the more cautious model of "a
fusion of horizons," the horizon of the text and that of the
reader (*DD*, 41).

Gadamer's model for the act of understanding is the conversation, the dialogue, the give-and-take that occurs between
the subject and the text, along with the ongoing process of
differentiation that takes place in this exchange. This, he argues, produces coherences, contexts, even systematic corre-
spondences, and thus identities.[8] For Gadamer, interpretation
consists in formulating, with the greatest possible rigor, the
response that the meeting with the text calls forth in us. In
agreement with the early Heidegger, Gadamer describes this
conception of the text as a "sketch" of meaning that begins "as
soon as a first meaning appears in the text" (*WM*, 370–71). At
the outset this image is only a "rough draft," constantly under
revision by new and "rival sketches," so that the "movement of
meaning in understanding and interpretation" amounts to a
"constant resketching," until "the unity of the meaning can
unequivocally be determined" (*WM*, 370–71). Even in the case
of an interpreter like Heidegger, who aggressively took pos-
session of texts, raped, and mutilated them, it can be shown
that his interpretation of Nietzsche did not result in a single,
compact assertion but took shape during a period of over ten
years through various new attempts and points of entry that
cannot necessarily be brought into a single line.

Hermeneutics would nevertheless appear, if Derrida's dis-

---

[8]See, in addition to the text of Gadamer's lecture "Text and Interpretation" (*DD*, 21–51), the following writings by Gadamer: "Der eminente Text
und seine Wahrheit," *Sprache und Literatur in Wissenschaft und Unterricht* 57
(1986): 4–10; "Dekonstruktion und Hermeneutik," in his *Gesammelte Werke*
(Tübingen: Mohr, 1986), 2: 361–72; and "Frühromantik, Hermeneutik, De-
konstruktivismus," in *Die Aktualität der Frühromantik*, ed. Ernst Behler and
Jochen Hörisch (Paderborn: Schöningh, 1987), 251–60.

tinctions were applied, as a procedure that operates with concepts like progressive connection, gradual integration, an emerging totality, enlargement of the context, ongoing continuity, coherence, and a developing congruence, all in relation to a somewhat removed totality. Its concept of unity would include difference but in the style of a dialogical structure organized around unanimity and understanding, even if the complete realization of meaning is unfulfilled in the present, remains obscure in the past, and will not be fully achieved in the future. The beliefs in congruity and a prevailing relation among all parts are constantly involved in such a perspective. The structural model of totality, unity, and a universal connection is fundamentally upheld.

Hermeneutics itself, from within the perspective of this structural model, assumes not only the individual act of understanding but also the process of understanding within individual disciplines, human history, and the lifeworld in general as an overarching context of meaning. It thus remains committed to metaphysical thinking. Without elaborating the commitment in detail, we could say that a certain relationship exists between hermeneutics and the notorious umbrella, since hermeneutics delivers "umbrella concepts" for all this. Above all, however, hermeneutics has interpreted its own activity as a procedure working with systematic connections, lived contexts, horizons, and world horizons, as well as representing its own history as the progressive achievement of meaning. Recent assessments of philosophical hermeneutics characterize the formation of contemporary hermeneutics as occurring in several teleologically related steps or phases. The process seems to have begun with the formation of Romantic hermeneutics as the first step into modernity. The phases are associated with the names of Schleiermacher (Romantic hermeneutics), Dilthey (the foundation of the humanities), the early Heidegger (the ontological turn), and Gadamer (the claim of the universality of hermeneutics). Other names are occasionally added to this sequence.

By contrast the names of writers like Nietzsche and Freud, who are no less important for the interpretation of texts but who did not share the metaphysical views underlying this tradition, are excluded from the tradition or abandoned in silence. This tactic can be seen most clearly in the case of Friedrich Schlegel, who could with good reasons appear as the one who initiated the Romantic turning point in the history of hermeneutics.[9] In fact, Schlegel's model of understanding rejected systematic connections; it was instead a procedure in which "incomprehensibility," "positive non-understanding," "confusion," and chaos played a decisive role. Indeed, Schlegel maintained his model explicitly in opposition to the ideas of the complete intelligibility of the world and absolute knowledge found in German idealism, which for him was represented above all by Hegel. "Truly," Schlegel wrote in the *Athenaeum*, "it would frighten you if the entire world seriously became comprehensible, as you demand it."[10] Schlegel ridiculed the hermeneutic tendency of placing an author or a text in a larger context as the theory of "better understanding" and joked about this model.[11] The irony of the situation was that Schleiermacher turned precisely this claim, of understanding an author better than he had understood himself, into a motto of the Romantic hermeneutics from which Schlegel was excluded.[12]

[9] See Hendrik Birus, "Hermeneutische Wende? Anmerkungen zur Schleiermacher-Interpretation," *Euphorion* 74 (1980): 213–21.

[10] *Kritische Friedrich Schlegel Ausgabe*, ed. Ernst Behler with Jean-Jacques Anstett and Hans Eichner, vol. 2, ed. Hans Eichner (Paderborn: Schöningh, 1967), 370.

[11] See Ernst Behler, "Friedrich Schlegels Theorie des Verstehens: Hermeneutik oder Dekonstruktion?," in *Die Aktualität der Frühromantik* (cited in note 8 to this chapter), 141–60.

[12] See Manfred Frank, "Die Bedeutung des Grundsatzes 'Einen Autor besser verstehen als er sich verstand,'" in idem, *Das individuelle Allgemeine: Textstrukturierung und -interpretation nach Schleiermacher* (Frankfurt: Suhrkamp, 1977), 358–64. In my opinion Schlegel's position is inverted here and turned into Schleiermacher's.

The program of "better understanding" was joined to other issues, for example, the psychology of unconscious creation and geniality. For Schlegel, however, these issues had little resonance.

In all likelihood, of course, Derrida did not have these moments from the history of modern hermeneutics in mind when he questioned the allegiance to a continuous context and the progressive enlargement of coherence and confronted these allegiances with an interpretive procedure punctuated by disruptive or discontinuous restructuring. But with Schlegel's concepts of incomprehensibility, confusion, and positive nonunderstanding, together with Nietzsche's unending interpretation, other models emerge that illustrate the specific character of Derrida's concept of interpretation.

Derrida first expressed this critical dispute with hermeneutics fully in his lecture on Heidegger's interpretation of Nietzsche. I explained why Derrida probably chose the topic, which led him beyond the context of the discussion on text and interpretation. It was meant to show, through a prominent example, how the hermeneutic operation functions. Derrida could as well have chosen Hölderlin, Rilke, Trakl, or any other chapter from the "history of Being." His concentration on Nietzsche, however, had an important purpose unconnected to Gadamer, for whom Nietzsche has never been of central importance.[13] Within contemporary German philosophy, people had begun to associate Nietzsche closely with contemporary French philosophy, in particular Foucault, Lyotard, and Derrida. This view is quite understandable, since these writers responded significantly to Nietzsche and contributed substantially to the creation of the "new Nietzsche," as the post-Heideggerian Nietzsche has been called.

But contemporary German philosophy saw the critique of reason and the self-critique of philosophy articulated by Nietz-

[13]See Hans-Georg Gadamer, "Das Drama Zarathustras," *Nietzsche-Studien* 15 (1986): 1–15.

sche (among others) as an essential threat, a radical attack on reason and thus on philosophy proper. The first signs of a counter-critique appear in a 1980 speech by Jürgen Habermas entitled "Modernity—An Incomplete Project," as well as in several essays by Habermas on the critique of reason by Horkheimer, Adorno, and Nietzsche.[14] With these writings Habermas sought to answer "the challenge from the neostructuralist critique of reason" raised by the three contemporary French writers. Habermas addressed the theme of a critique of reason and the self-critique of philosophy through the perspective of larger historical contexts. In the earlier programmatic lecture on the "incomplete project" of modernity, he saw the "postmodern" critique of reason undertaken by French philosophy as fundamentally anti-modern, an attempt to sacrifice the rational tradition of modernity in order to make room for a new "historicism" and to rebel against everything normative. The lecture discusses primarily aesthetic modernity, but it also deals to a certain extent with the separation of the cultural spheres of science, morality, and art in the modern world. Habermas would like to find a new connection, to establish a rational linkage, among these spheres, a goal that brings him close to the metaphysical commitments of philosophical hermeneutics.

For our purpose, however, the particularly important question raised by Habermas is whether we want to follow the intentions of the Enlightenment, as weak as they may seem, or whether we see the entire project of modernity as a lost game. Of course, Habermas's answer consisted in a belief in "communicative rationality" and a commitment to the values and norms of the Enlightenment. Hence he characterized the "postmodern" critique of this position as the false negation of culture and satirized the representatives of such a critique in

---

[14] Jürgen Habermas, "Modernity—An Incomplete Project," in *The Anti-Aesthetic: Essays on Postmodern Culture*, ed. Hal Foster (Port Townsend, Wash.: Bay Press, 1983), 3–15. The other essays were collected later in *DM*.

an obscure polemic as "neo-conservatives," or "young conservatives." He described them as a "line" running from Georges Bataille through Michel Foucault to Derrida. With this suggestion, he joined all the participants in the dispute between hermeneutics and deconstruction in one line of descent.[15] The revelations of these authors reflect, according to Habermas, a decentered subjectivity that has removed itself from the demands of work and utility and stands outside the modern world. They confront "instrumental reason" with a principle that can be reached only by evocations of, for example, the will to power or sovereignty, Being, or the Dionysian power of the poetic.

Understandably this counter-critique is no longer carried out in the style of Georg Lukacs ("The Destruction of Reason from Schelling to Hitler").[16] However, in its unspecified black-and-white images, its globalizing linearity, the application of clichés such as "irrationalism" and "nihilism," and above all the use of political and "ideologically critical" categories like "conservatism," the discourse of Habermas bears a surprising resemblance to Lukacs's. In particular, Habermas tried later in *The Philosophical Discourse of Modernity* to attach to the thought of most of these authors, including Nietzsche, a religious dimension that supposedly corresponded to their "conservatism." Since he did, in fact, construct a "line" of irrationality from Friedrich Schlegel's "Discourse on Mythology" through Nietzsche to Derrida (*DM*, 88–92), it appears that he failed to read these authors sufficiently in terms of their own specific concerns and that by linking these authors too closely in a kind of "wave thinking" he had transferred too much of Schlegel to the others. For as Nietzsche said of Schlegel in light of an anecdote about Goethe, Schlegel was in danger of "suf-

[15]For Derrida's response, see "Antwort an Apel" (cited in note 1 to this chapter).

[16]Georg Lukacs, *Die Zerstörung der Vernunft*, 3 vols. (Darmstadt and Neuwied, 1973).

focating from the regurgitation of moral and religious absur-
dities" (*KSA*, 13: 495). As I mentioned earlier, Habermas
has—in all seriousness—characterized Derrida as a "Jewish
mystic" searching for a lost super-script, an enterprise meant
presumably as a substitute for Heidegger's unrealizable philosophy of origins (*DM*, 161–84). It is at this point presumably
unnecessary to consider these and other misunderstandings,
about which Derrida himself has written.[17]

One other classifying type of approach was initiated by
Manfred Frank, with his attempt to reduce Derrida's deconstructive and disseminating text interpretations to the
hermeneutics of Schleiermacher.[18] Frank also argued that
Schleiermacher had achieved the same results more convincingly, because he had avoided the "hysterical" thesis of
the loss of the subject.[19] Frank's polemic acts as if it had
never occurred to Nietzsche and Derrida that our attempts—
through every means of self-critique—to overcome individuality and subjectivity in the form of anthropomorphism, psy-
chologism, or transcendentalism, as well as the attempt to suspend every determinate version of human beings in either a
singular or plural form, would not be successful, since inevitably we fall back into human, all too human, forms of intui-

[17]Jacques Derrida, "Positionen, 14 Jahre später," in idem, *Positionen: Ge-
spräche mit Henri Ronse, Julia Kristeva, Jean-Louis Houdebine, Guy Scarpetta*,
ed. Peter Engelmann (Vienna: Passagen, 1986), 9–30; "Gespräch mit Jacques
Derrida," in *Philosophien*, ed. Peter Engelmann (Vienna: Passagen, 1985),
51–70; and "Antwort an Apel" (cited in note 1 to this chapter).

[18]See esp. Manfred Frank, *What Is Neostructuralism?*, trans. Sabine
Wilke and Richard Gray (Minneapolis: University of Minnesota Press, 1988).
See also Frank, *Das Sagbare und das Unsagbare: Studien zur neuesten fran-
zösischen Hermeneutik und Texttheorie* (Frankfurt: Suhrkamp, 1980).

[19]Manfred Frank, "Zwei Jahrhunderte Rationalitätskritik und ihre
'postmoderne' Überbietung," in *Die unvollendete Vernunft: Moderne versus
Postmoderne*, ed. Dietmar Kamper and Willem van Reijen (Frankfurt:
Suhrkamp, 1987), 99–121; Frank, *Die Unhintergehbarkeit von Individualität:
Reflexionen über Subjekt, Person und Individuum aus Anlass ihrer 'postmoder-
nen' Toterklärung* (Frankfurt: Suhrkamp, 1986).

tion and thought.[20] For Frank, such questions amount to an insult to the majesty of rationality and reason: "To question the legitimacy of rationality means nothing less than to place the authority whose name granted legitimacy under suspicion, even as something in need of legitimation."[21]

For Habermas, too, Nietzsche's writings formulate a critique of ideology designed to attack its own foundations. Now, the "two moments—that of reason and that of its other—stand not in an opposition pointing to a dialectical Aufhebung (sublimation), but in a relationship of tension characterized by mutual repugnance and exclusion" (*DM*, 103). Habermas evidently assumes that a critique of ideology which does not attack its own foundations and instead relies on Hegelian or Marxist dialectics would necessarily be better. In this view two trajectories govern the tradition: either the "philosophical mysticism" extending from the late Heidegger to Derrida, or the "theory of power" from Bataille to Foucault (*DM*, 104). But for both lines, as well as for Nietzsche, Horkheimer, and Adorno, a situation emerges that Habermas describes in monstrous terms: "The totalizing self-critique of reason gets caught in a performative contradiction since it can convict subject-centered reason of being authoritarian in nature only by having recourse to reason's own tools" (*DM*, 185). The philosophical relevance of Nietzsche, Adorno, and Derrida is called into question through a narrow, departmentalized perspective. Habermas suggests that critical philosophical problems could be dismissed through simplistic, sarcastic remarks and that these could form the basis for the authority and legitimacy of rationality.

To conclude this analysis, I will discuss the concepts of unity

[20]But see Nietzsche, "Let us beware" (*GS*, 167–69): "When will we complete our de-deification of nature? When may we begin to 'naturalize' humanity in terms of a pure, newly discovered, newly redeemed nature?"; and Derrida, "The Ends of Man," in *MP*, 109–36.

[21]Manfred Frank, "Zwei Jahrhunderte Rationalitätskritik" (cited in note 19 to this chapter), 99.

and totality, which play a decisive role in the discussion of hermeneutics and lead more specifically back to Nietzsche. The ending of Derrida's essay "Interpreting Signatures" considers the problem of totality in the context of a model of disruptive or discontinuous re-structuration and states his view of totality in explicit contrast to Heidegger's unifying interpretation of Nietzsche's text.

The argument can be explained from the course of the debate. Gadamer stated that Derrida's conception of understanding as "a breach, a *rupture*," and *not* as a "continuous understanding of another person" (*DD*, 56), does not offer a genuine alternative to his own concept of understanding but simply forms a subspecies of universal hermeneutics. Such a breach could be characterized with Heidegger as a "blow [*Stoss*]," "which thrusts itself upon us," and thus in no way assumes "the reassuring confirmation of mutual agreement" (*DD*, 57). It concerns rather the "experience of limits that we encounter in our life with others," insofar as it reveals the possibility of more than "common interests" (*DD*, 57). But even with the disruptions, we absorb the text at the same time, we accept it, and we begin "a long and often repeated effort at understanding" (*DD*, 57). In Gadamer's view, such a moment "not only strikes us and deals us a blow but also is supposed to be accepted," for "one must lose oneself in order to find oneself" (*DD*, 57).

Once again, Gadamer's account is organized around the hermeneutic principle of a non-present, removed totality; this distantiation nevertheless maintains the priority of totality, unity, and an underlying context. Derrida would have to show that his disruptive principle of interpretation is not only slightly different from a totalizing model but thoroughly different structurally. A similar attempt to determine the difference from the progressively unifying model can be found in the long footnote with which Habermas ends his chapter on Derrida in *The Philosophical Discourse of Modernity*. Habermas describes the resistance of Heidegger, Adorno, and Derrida to the principles of rationality: "They all still defend themselves as if they were living in the shadow of the 'last' philosopher, as did the first generation of Hegelian disciples. They are still battling against the 'strong' concepts of theory, truth, and system that have actually belonged to the past for over a century and a half" (*DM*, 408). They believe, in other words, that they "have to tear philosophy away from the madness of expounding a theory that has the last word" (*DM*, 408). If this did in fact need to be done, "then an *adequate* critique of reason would really have to grasp the roots at such a depth that it could scarcely avoid the paradoxes of self-referentiality" (*DM*, 408). In reality, according to Habermas, contemporary philosophy no longer expects an "unconditional validity or 'ultimate foundations,'" but works with "fallibilist consciousness" and truth claims at the same time (*DM*, 408–9). That is, philosophy has adjusted to the likelihood that its theories will have to be revised: "It prefers a combination of strong propositions with weak status claims; so little is this totalitarian, that there is no call for a totalizing critique of reason against it" (*DM*, 409).

As in philosophical hermeneutics, Habermas endorses the model of the self-enlarging context as a revised, "weak" model of totalization. To distinguish Derrida's position, one could return to the essay on Lévi-Strauss, particularly the discussion of structuralism, in which Derrida contrasted two kinds of totalizing strategies. For Derrida, both strategies are "impossible," a judgment he could apply either to the revisionist Hegelianism of communications theory or to philosophical hermeneutics.[22] One kind of totalization can be judged as impossible "in the classical style: one then refers to the empirical endeavor of either a subject or a finite richness which it can never master" (*WD*, 289). Another kind of "nontotalization" can also be determined, not from the awareness of the finitude of our perspectives but on the basis of a structural impossibility;

[22] Jacques Derrida, "Structure, Sign and Play in the Discourse of the Human Sciences," *WD*, 289.

namely, we ourselves are involved in a field of play on which
infinite substitutions can occur, and yet no center, no ground,
will be provided. The "movement of *supplementarity*" is never
exhausted, insofar as "there is always more" (*WD*, 289).
One could also explain this difference using Derrida's concept of play and contrast his concept with the continuity found
in all Hegelian-style interpretations, that is, according to the
principle of "logical continuity." Derrida has in fact done this
himself. As he wrote in one of his studies of Hegel:

The necessity of *logical* continuity is the decision or interpretive milieu of all Hegelian interpretations. In interpreting negativity as la-
bor, in betting for discourse, meaning, history, etc., Hegel has bet
against play, against chance. He has blinded himself to the possibility
of his own bet, to the fact that the conscientious suspension of play
(for example, the movement through the certitude of oneself and
through lordship to the independence of self-consciousness) was itself
a phase of play; and to the fact that play includes the work of meaning or the meaning of work, and includes them not in terms of
knowledge, but in terms of inscription: meaning is a function of play,
is inscribed in a certain place in the configuration of a meaningless play.   (*WD*, 260)

In the context of the German-French debate, Derrida returns to the Heideggerian interpretation of Nietzsche to illustrate the fundamental difference between his conception of totality and Heidegger's reading of Nietzsche. It should suffice
to emphasize one point of dispute. Based on numerous passages in Nietzsche's writing, Derrida concludes that he "by no
means trusts any thought of totality" and that even the "reference to the 'totality of beings'" does not play the "structuring
role" for Nietzsche that it does for Heidegger (*DD*, 69). Hence,
for example, the thought of the eternal recurrence is "not a
thought about totality" as Heidegger would have it, and Nietzsche's numerous statements about life and death are by no
means subordinate "to an unequivocal meaning of totality, of
the relation between a whole and a non-whole" (*DD*, 70). Just
as Nietzsche suggests that life should be thought from death,

he recommends in another passage "to think the word 'being' starting from life and not the other way around" (*DD*, 71). Derrida summarizes this kind of thinking: "There, opposition or contradiction no longer constitutes a law dictating prohibitions to thought. And that without dialectic" (*DD*, 71). At this point Derrida turns to Nietzsche's warning in the aphorism "Let us beware" in *The Gay Science* (*GS*, 167–69): "Let us beware of saying that death is opposed to life. The living is merely a type of what is dead, and a very rare type" (*GS*, 168). For Derrida, "Nietzsche thwarts all that governs the thought or even the anticipation of totality, namely, the relationship of genus and species" (*DD*, 71). He endorses instead "a unique inclusion—without any possible totalization—of the 'whole' in the 'part,' with a metonymizing free from limits" (*DD*, 71). Derrida condenses Nietzsche's deconstruction of totality: "Without protection! Let us protect ourselves against all protections [*Gardons-nous du garde-fou*]" (*TUI*, 86).

TRANSLATOR'S AFTERWORD

Nietzsche in North America: Walter Kaufmann and After

From the preceding analysis it could be inferred that Western culture in the twentieth century has unfolded as a discontinuous series of confrontations with Nietzsche. Of course it may be premature to say that, from the predominantly literary response around the turn of the twentieth century to the increasing interest among contemporary philosophers, the Western world has experienced, as Allan Bloom describes it, the "Nietzscheanization" of culture in general (C, 217). Nevertheless it does seem, from Martin Heidegger to Jacques Derrida, that a decisive shift has occurred in the self-understanding of continental European philosophy, and that this shift has repeatedly been articulated in response to Nietzsche. The critique of metaphysics has become, more broadly and more intensively, an "auto-critique of philosophy." By describing the several features of such a shift, the preceding genealogy also contributes to the critique.[1] This Afterword is meant to extend the critique to the North American debate.[2]

[1] As such, this genealogy shares in the project of a descriptive critique with others that have appeared recently, for example, the analysis by Allan Megill, *Prophets of Extremity: Nietzsche, Heidegger, Foucault, Derrida* (Berkeley: University of California Press, 1985).

[2] See, for an earlier and somewhat different account, Bernd Magnus,

Striking parallels exist between the reception of Nietzsche in continental Europe and the reception in North America. Just as the continental image of Nietzsche was dominated in the 1960's and 1970's by Heidegger's interpretation, the North American image was dominated by Walter Kaufmann. Moreover, in both contexts the writings of Maurice Blanchot, Jacques Derrida, Sarah Kofman, Pierre Klossowski, Philippe Lacoue-Labarthe, Jean-Luc Nancy, and Bernard Pautrat played a major role in the subsequent creation of a "new Nietzsche," a writer of previously unrecognized deconstructive capacity.[3] The "other" Nietzsche is the one who, in Derrida's terms, "is no longer turned toward the origin, affirms play and tries to pass beyond man and humanism," who disrupts the coherence of the system and the center of a structure (*WD*, 292).

Yet despite the broad similarities connecting the continental European to the North American receptions of Nietzsche, which at times suggest that a single, Amero-european field has emerged, numerous differences remain. The different shape of Nietzsche's image in English is due largely to the efforts of Walter Kaufmann. Whereas Heidegger's interpretation, with its emphasis on "the will to power" and "the eternal recurrence of the same" as two sides of the same unifying principle, dominated the postwar reception of Nietzsche in Europe, Kaufmann's interpretation shaped the reception in English from 1950 to at least 1974, or for nearly a quarter of a century. In the four editions of *Nietzsche: Philosopher, Psychologist, Antichrist*, through his writings on the history of philosophy and literature, and especially through his translations of numerous Nietzsche texts, which still form the basis of most English readers' image of Nietzsche, he consistently developed the

---

"Nietzsche Today: A View from America," *International Studies in Philosophy* 15, 2 (1983): 95–103.

[3]Cf. David B. Allison, ed., *The New Nietzsche* (cited in note 1 to the Introduction).

point he had made in 1950: "The will to power *is* the core of Nietzsche's thought, but inseparable from his idea of sublimation" (*NPPA*, xiv). His contention determined the image of Nietzsche in English until the 1970's; since then it has sparked considerable debate.

Sublimation, as Kaufmann conceived it, involves the process of self-overcoming. According to Kaufmann, Nietzsche's "intentions are singularly unequivocal, and he was not one to sit on both sides of the fence at once. Insofar as he had a 'dual nature,' he was seeking to overcome it: 'My strongest characteristic is self-overcoming.' Self-overcoming, not ambiguity, is the key to Nietzsche" (*NPPA*, 16). To a certain extent, Kaufmann's arguments arise as modifications of Karl Jaspers's work. Jaspers had seen the importance of the contradictory or "dual nature" for Nietzsche and had recognized self-overcoming as an important moment in Nietzsche's thought, but the process of self-overcoming for Jaspers became—from Kaufmann's perspective—vague, endless, and self-defeating. Nietzsche's more specific concerns, "in the sense of clearly defined questions capable of being answered, are neglected, and Jaspers may be said to revert to Stefan George's poetic vision" (*NPPA*, 16). Kaufmann situated his own work as building upon and refining Jaspers's: now, Nietzsche's central problems could be addressed and his answers given.

To understand Nietzsche's "problems and solutions," Kaufmann argued, it is necessary to see them "separately from the survey of his life, as any joint treatment will almost inevitably suggest a false notion of causal relationship between life and philosophy" (*NPPA*, 21). Nietzsche's life, including his family background, his schooling, his relations with Wagner and Lou Andreas-Salome, and finally his illness, should not be seen as having any strictly causal relation to the work (*NPPA*, 70). A clear judgment of Nietzsche's significance can be achieved only, in Kaufmann's view, "by a careful examination of his thought" (*NPPA*, 71).

At this point the similarities of Kaufmann's reading to Heidegger's can be seen: just as Kaufmann relegated the biographical information to a less prominent position, so Heidegger criticized "the psychological-biological addiction of our times" (*N*, 1: 10). For both, the biography was far less important than the thought, even if the thought emphasized the most intimate details of the life, including dental and eating disorders.[4] Heidegger and Kaufmann also agreed on the importance of the will to power theme: for both, it was a central thread running through Nietzsche's argument. Both created an image of Nietzsche organized around a central theme, and both explored the oscillations of Nietzsche's texts in relation to that center.

Nevertheless, the differences between their respective positions are more significant than the similarities. A decisive difference involves the relation of Nietzsche's texts to his philosophy. For Heidegger, Nietzsche's most important thoughts do not appear in any of the texts published in his lifetime: "Nietzsche's philosophy proper, the fundamental position on the basis of which he speaks in these and in all the writings he himself published, did not assume a final form and was not itself published in any book, neither in the decade between 1879 and 1889 nor during the years preceding" (*N*, 1: 8–9). Heidegger then privileged the fragments and aphorisms collected as *The Will to Power*. For Kaufmann, however, although the theme of the will to power is central, it can be understood only "against the background of his total literary output" (*NPPA*, 8). When the bulk of Nietzsche's texts, especially the published ones, are included in the analysis, the will to power is seen neither as a metaphysical nor as an ontological construction, Kaufmann argues, but "first and foremost [as] the key concept of a

[4]Though at least two illuminating biographies have been written in English: Ronald Hayman, *Nietzsche: A Critical Life* (New York: Oxford University Press, 1980); and R. J. Hollingdale, *Nietzsche: The Man and His Philosophy* (Baton Rouge: Louisiana State University Press, 1965).

psychological hypothesis" (*NPPA*, 204). Thus Kaufmann, in an explicit rejection of Heidegger's argument, asserts that the will to power must be seen "as a universal feature of the human constitution" (*NPPA*, 206), and he organizes his position toward what Derrida ironically calls "the unity of human-reality" (*MP*, 115). In describing Nietzsche's view of the structures of human reality, Kaufmann provides a detailed and comprehensive, humanistic-anthropological reading. This purpose also guides Kaufmann's editions and translations of the texts. In the translator's afterword to *The Will to Power*, for example, Kaufmann dismisses the notebooks as "of secondary interest" and emphasizes again the importance of the books Nietzsche published in his lifetime: "For all my interest in Nietzsche, I still believe as firmly as ever that the books he finished are his legacy, and that his notebooks are of secondary interest—as I explained in section I of the second chapter of my *Nietzsche*."[5] In contrast to Heidegger and Derrida, Kaufmann would overlook both the notebooks published as *The Will to Power* and fragments such as "I have lost my umbrella," or, primarily, the texts of the *Nachlass*.[6] As a result, although he translated many Nietzsche texts, Kaufmann also overlooked several, some of them very long, which have in the meantime become important in Nietzsche research, including

[5]Friedrich Nietzsche, *The Will to Power*, trans. Walter Kaufmann and R. J. Hollingdale (New York: Random House, 1967), 551–52.

[6]The "uses and abuses" of the *Nachlass* have frequently been a central issue in the reception of Nietzsche. Recently, Bernd Magnus distinguished between "lumpers" and "splitters" on the basis of their evaluation of the *Nachlass*: "Lumpers are drawn to Nietzsche's *Nachlass*, to his literary estate. . . . Splitters, in contrast to lumpers, tend to distinguish sharply between published and unpublished writings in Nietzsche's case." For Magnus, Kaufmann "was a special case in this taxonomy. He generally claimed to be a splitter but in practice was frequently a lumper." See Magnus, "The Use and Abuse of *The Will to Power*," in *Reading Nietzsche*, ed. Robert C. Solomon and Kathleen M. Higgins (New York: Oxford University Press, 1988), 218–35; quotation at 220–21.

"Truth and Lie in an Extra-Moral Sense," the *Untimely Meditations, Human, All Too Human, Daybreak*, and the early *Philologica*. These particular texts avoid or resist the themes of self-overcoming and the will to power.

The translations themselves are organized to support Kaufmann's interpretation. This is most visible in some of the footnotes added to the texts, which in certain instances produce a running commentary. One example is the note to Aphorism 2, Book One, of *The Gay Science*, which uses the aphorism to reject various interpretations of Nietzsche: "Many interpretations of Nietzsche's thought are invalidated by this very important and characteristic section. Nietzsche never renounced it" (*GS*, 77). Another tendency of the footnotes is to refer often to specific pages in Kaufmann's *Nietzsche* for support, or to criticize the distortions and mistranslations of other translators. Several footnotes of both types appear, for example, in the translation of the *Genealogy of Morals* and *Ecce Homo* (*GM*, 40–41). In general, however, Kaufmann highlights the terms most central to his interpretation. One of the more pronounced instances occurs in the translation of the *Genealogy*, in the footnote concerning the phrase "sich selbst aufhebend," or "overcoming itself," as Kaufmann renders it:

Aufheben is a very troublesome word, though common in ordinary German. Literally, it means "pick up"; but it has two derivative meanings that are no less common: "cancel" and "preserve" or "keep." Something picked up is no longer there, but the point of picking it up may be to keep it. Hegel made much of this term; his use of it is explained and discussed in Walter Kaufmann, *Hegel* (Garden City, N.Y., Doubleday, 1965; Garden City, N.Y., Doubleday, Anchor Books, 1966), section 34—and a comparison of Hegel and Nietzsche on this point may be found in Kaufmann's *Nietzsche*, Chapter 8, section II.   (*GM*, 73)

Together with the humanistic-anthropological emphasis, Kaufmann's interpretation and translations consistently emphasize the Hegelian element in Nietzsche's texts.

From these characterizations, it can be surmised how different Kaufmann's image of Nietzsche is from those of Foucault, Deleuze, and Derrida. Yet despite the sharp differences between Kaufmann's image and those resisting Nietzsche's "psychology," there is at least one point of intersection: the theme of masks. Especially in his later book *Discovering the Mind*, Kaufmann considers Nietzsche's "final contribution" to be his "philosophy of masks" (*DTM*, 137). Kaufmann draws particular attention to the importance of *Verstellung* ("dissimulation," "irony") for Nietzsche (*DTM*, 140) and relates these themes to that of "role playing" (*DTM*, 142). At first these themes seem closely related and would bring Kaufmann's Nietzsche close to Derrida's with its emphasis on signs, infinite play, and shifting interpretation. But Kaufmann reasserts the importance of a developmental and historical perspective for Nietzsche and places him closer to Goethe than to Heidegger: "Nietzsche thinks in terms of development, like Goethe" (*DTM*, 143).

Kaufmann's systematic and multifaceted work dominated the English-language reception of Nietzsche for nearly twenty-five years and retains a considerable impact. Its basic features are an emphasis on the completed texts published during Nietzsche's lifetime, strategies of editing and translation that highlight the themes of the will to power and self-overcoming, and a related constellation of themes including the psychological constitution of human nature, personal development, and an evolutionary historical interpretation. This perspective represses the contradictions in Nietzsche's writing in favor of coherence and avoids the problematic political statements in favor of a pervasively anthropological, nearly Hegelian humanism. Although Kaufmann's views have been prominent, they have also provoked challenges at almost every point.

The challenges to Kaufmann's perspective have emerged from two primary directions and have hinged upon a pivotal question, one that has been called "the question of style."[7] That is, do Nietzsche's texts, which contain different kinds of writing, develop on the basis of general principles and systematic coherence? Writers such as Arthur C. Danto, Bernd Magnus, and Richard Schacht have argued in favor of general principles and an underlying systematic coherence to Nietzsche's writing. These writers have cast an image of "Nietzsche as philosopher," to use Danto's phrase, but base his philosophical teachings on principles different from Kaufmann's.[8] The preface to Danto's book signals the change in reception most clearly:

> I shall take Nihilism as the central concept in his philosophy, and through it I shall try to show the connections, altogether systematic, among those exotic doctrines that otherwise loom so blankly out of the surrounding aphorisms and frantic obiter dicta. I shall even endeavor to show that these obiter dicta are neither the surface nor the substance of what he had to say, but rather illustrations and applications of certain general principles to particular cases. Finally, I hope to locate these general principles in the main philosophical tradition, as proposed answers to the same problems that have occupied the best attention of philosophers throughout the ages.   (22)

Danto's position can be contrasted to Kaufmann's. From this perspective, Nietzsche's writing is systematic, governed by principles, and proposes answers to ancient problems, but the system and its principles are different from the will to power and the overcoming of the self. For Danto, the central concept is "Nihilism," capitalized in order to emphasize its importance. The several other themes of Nietzsche's writing, for example, art and irrationality, perspectivism, psychology, the *Übermensch*, eternal recurrence, and the will to power, are funda-

---

[7]Alan D. Schrift marks the "question of style" as a "focal point in the interpretation of Nietzsche's text." See his *Nietzsche and the Question of Interpretation: Between Hermeneutics and Deconstruction* (New York: Routledge, 1990), 82.

[8]See Arthur C. Danto, *Nietzsche as Philosopher* (New York: Macmillan, 1965). Cited directly in the text.

mentally related to philosophical nihilism in this "philosophy behind the philosophy, the meaning masked by the words" (231). Danto's book marked a significant turning point for the reception of Nietzsche in North America. In contrast to Kaufmann's psychological and religious treatment, Danto suggested that Nietzsche foreshadowed many of the problems and arguments of analytic, Anglo-American philosophy. It was against this suggestion in particular that Walter Kaufmann argued: "We should resist the fashionable tendency to assimilate German philosophers by claiming that they really said what some recent British and American philosophers have said, too. If we admit what is foreign and different only after showing to our satisfaction that it is not different or new after all, we gain nothing, and we destroy all incentives for studying non-English texts" (*NPPA*, 423).

But it was that very "foreignness" and "difference" in Nietzsche's writing which compelled Bernd Magnus and Richard Schacht to recommend different general principles as the organizing centers of Nietzsche's project. Bernd Magnus, in contrast to Kaufmann and Danto, emphasized the doctrine of eternal recurrence as Nietzsche's "self-confessed principal idea."[9] With the notion of eternal recurrence as the "principal idea," Magnus subsequently argues a twin thesis in his book on Nietzsche. First, "the doctrine of eternal recurrence is a visual and conceptual representation of the being-in-the-world of an *Übermensch*" (xiii). As a representation, it articulates or portrays certain attitudes toward life and even a certain form of life. These attitudes are the opposite of decadence and stress

[9]See Magnus, *Nietzsche's Existential Imperative* (cited in note 15 to Chapter 3), xiii. See also the treatments of the eternal recurrence in a number of other recent authors, including Arthur Danto, *Nietzsche as Philosopher* (cited in note 8 to this chapter), 195–213; Ivan Soll, "Reflections on Recurrence," in *Nietzsche: A Collection of Critical Essays*, ed. Robert Solomon (Garden City, N.Y.: Doubleday, 1973), 343–57; and Joan Stambaugh, *Nietzsche's Thought of Eternal Return* (Baltimore: Johns Hopkins University Press, 1972).

affirmation above all.[10] That form of life which most clearly embodies such affirmation is the *Übermensch*.[11]

Second, Magnus sees Nietzsche's doctrine of eternal recurrence in "the form of an eternalistic countermyth" (xiv). It is "eternalist" in the sense of praising, as eternality has been understood from Plato to Hegel. Nietzsche's praise is seen as the consecration of a "countermyth," or a "counterhypothesis," a position that celebrates experience or becoming: "He sought to overcome this traditional retreat from transient experience, represented by metaphysics, Christianity, and nihilism within a single formulation; the doctrine of eternal recurrence" (xiv). For Magnus, Nietzsche offers the radical affirmation of transitory human experience despite suffering and death.

By contrast, Richard Schacht, in his book on *Nietzsche* and in a later article "Nietzsche's *Gay Science*," emphasizes "human life and possibility" as his "point of departure and constant return."[12] For Schacht, Nietzsche replaces epistemology and metaphysics "by a kind of *philosophical anthropology* as the fundamental and central philosophical endeavor" (72). Nietzsche's main effort, both in *The Gay Science* and elsewhere, was to "complete our de-deification of nature" and "to 'naturalize' humanity" (76). Moreover, Nietzsche's concern with human nature is of a type related to Hegel and even Kant (79). What all three share is the intention to enhance our understanding

---

[10]Nietzsche's affirmative thought has consistently been an important topic in the reception. See Yirmiyahu Yovel, ed., *Nietzsche as Affirmative Thinker* (Dordrecht: Martinus Nijhoff, 1986).

[11]For more on Magnus's view of the *Übermensch*, see his later article "Perfectibility and Attitude in Nietzsche's *Übermensch*" (cited in note 14 to Chapter 3), which suggests that in some respects Magnus argues from a position close to that of both Derrida and Rorty.

[12]See Richard Schacht, *Nietzsche* (London: Routledge & Kegan Paul, 1983), esp. chap. 5, "Man and Men" (267–340); and "Nietzsche's *Gay Science*, Or, How to Naturalize Cheerfully," in *Reading Nietzsche*, ed. Robert C. Solomon and Kathleen M. Higgins (New York: Oxford University Press, 1988), 68–86; quotation at 72; cited directly in the text.

of ourselves so as to enable "further transformation" (80). They, and especially Nietzsche, remain committed to the possibility of attaining a "higher humanity" (80). This argument explicitly resists Foucault: "Far from thinking that the end of metaphysics and the critique of the disciplines Foucault scrutinizes preclude anything like a philosophical anthropology, Nietzsche writes as though they open the way for such inquiry to assume stage front and center in philosophy" (84). From Kaufmann to Danto, Magnus, and Schacht, in other words, arguments are constructed in favor of the systematic coherence of Nietzsche's writing, but in each case organized around a center of a different name. A discontinuous "series of substitutions of center for center," as Derrida might describe it, appears to have taken place (*WD*, 279).

Since the publication of Derrida's *Spurs* (1972), however, a second type of challenge to Kaufmann's interpretation of Nietzsche has emerged in response to the "question of style." The first type challenges Kaufmann with a variety of different principles, while nevertheless maintaining the search for a systematic coherence underlying Nietzsche's style; the second emphasizes the plurality of Nietzsche's style and resists the effort to establish an underlying unity.[13] Writers such as Alexander Nehamas and David Farrell Krell have explored this second direction and have reacted to a considerable extent to the swerves in the reception of Nietzsche added by Derrida, Sarah Kofman, and Pierre Klossowski.[14] In the process, a

[13] Interestingly, Danto early recognized the plural quality of Nietzsche's style: "Nietzsche's books give the impression of having been assembled rather than composed" (*Nietzsche as Philosopher* [cited in note 8 to this chapter], 19). But he criticized this plurality and saw it as ultimately resting on an underlying unity.

[14] For Nehamas, Kofman's most pertinent text is *Nietzsche et la métaphore* (Paris: Payot, 1972). For Krell, the relevant text by Klossowski is *Nietzsche et le cercle vicieux* (Paris: Mercure de France, 1969). An excerpt from the latter appears in David Allison, *The New Nietzsche* (cited in note 1 to the Introduction), 107–20.

markedly different image of Nietzsche has been constructed, namely, the image of "Nietzsche as writer."

Nehamas foregrounds the question of style in the very title of his book: *Nietzsche: Life as Literature*.[15] His point is that Nietzsche's writing explores many styles and that this stylistic plurality is important: "What I claim is simply that his stylistic variations play a crucial philosophical (or, from his point of view, antiphilosophical) role in his writing" (5). Whereas Kaufmann, in his effort to find an underlying unity behind or beneath Nietzsche's aphorisms, concentrated on the aphorism as the stylistic "heart of Nietzsche's writing," Nehamas draws attention to Nietzsche's remarkable use of different forms (14). There are, for example, notes (*The Will to Power*), the scholarly treatise (*The Birth of Tragedy*), the essay (*Untimely Meditations*), the polemical pamphlet (*The Case of Wagner*), autobiography (*Ecce Homo*), the many "lyric, epigrammatic, and dithyrambic poems," and "the vast number of letters, all of which belong to his writing as surely as every one of his aphorisms" (18–19). Nietzsche demonstrates through this stylistic pluralism "that writing is perhaps the most important part of thinking" (42). Indeed, Nehamas ultimately reaches the somewhat more radical conclusion implied by his title, namely, that for Nietzsche "writing is also the most important part of living" (42).

Such an interpretation rests on Nietzsche's basically literary model, and Nehamas uses this model to introduce the other dimensions of Nietzsche's thought. The first is Nietzsche's equivocal relation to philosophy, reflected in his ambiguous attitude toward Socrates. It is especially Socrates's dogmatism, or Plato's dogmatism through Socrates, that is objectionable to Nietzsche. In reaction Nietzsche posits and enacts a thoroughgoing perspectivism, which allows him to present views without having to insist that they are more than views of his own.

[15](Cambridge, Mass.: Harvard University Press, 1985). Cited directly in the text.

Thus he is able to distinguish his own practice from what he considers to be the dogmatic practice of earlier philosophers. The combination of stylistic variation, perspectivism, and the critique of traditional philosophy occurs, Nehamas argues, "in order to prevent his readers from overlooking the fact that his views necessarily originate with him. He depends on many styles in order to suggest that there is no single, neutral language in which his views, or any others, can ever be presented" (37). Here the contrast to Heidegger and to Kaufmann becomes clear, for Nehamas suggests that Nietzsche's life plays an important philosophical role in his writing. The stylistic pluralism of his writing combines with his perspectivism and the critique of philosophy in an effort to turn, as Nehamas puts it, "his life into literature" (234).

David Farrell Krell extends these lines of investigation in his recent *Of Memory, Reminiscence, and Writing: On the Verge*.[16] Whereas Nehamas considers the "question of style" for Nietzsche in tandem with Derrida and Sarah Kofman, Krell approaches the question with Derrida and Pierre Klossowski. From this perspective, Nietzsche's stylistic multiplicity introduces a number of different preoccupations, for example, "a flux and reflux of contradictory pulsions—bitterness, laughter, and silence," or "mirth and mourning, yes-saying and promise, but also contamination and hesitation" (282–83). In addition, however, and perhaps even more important, the work with Derrida and others leads Krell to transform his own writing style quite thoroughly. No longer, as in the texts of Kaufmann, Danto, Magnus, Schacht, and Nehamas, is there writing of a straightforward, declarative type; the reflection on writing produces a web of citations from various works of literature and philosophical writings. The result is a massive assemblage

[16](Bloomington: Indiana University Press, 1990); cited directly in the text. See also his *Postponements: Woman, Sensuality, and Death in Nietzsche* (Bloomington: Indiana University Press, 1986); and the volume he co-edited with David Wood, *Exceedingly Nietzsche: Aspects of Contemporary Nietzsche Interpretation* (London: Routledge & Kegan Paul, 1988).

of the most disparate kinds of materials, borrowed and manufactured, from the poetic to the philosophical, and across numerous eras.

Krell agrees with Nehamas that Nietzsche attempted to turn his life into literature, but he carries the consequences of this finding one step further. The distance between the discourse of the critic and the discourse of Nietzsche is alternately maintained and overcome, then coupled with citations from other texts: "In his own way, in the dramaturgic-genealogical theater of prehistory, Nietzsche *told me the bone would have to be broken again and inside me it began to say Ah Ah Ah and I began to sweat* recreates the story of memory as typography (5, 295): 'How shall a memory be made for the human animal? How shall one imprint something on this somewhat dull, somewhat flighty intellect-of-the-instant [*Augenblicks-Verstand*] and bit of embodied oblivion, so that it will remain present [*gegenwärtig*]?'" (274) Krell incorporates Nietzsche's writing into his own reflections on writing, memory, and reminiscence, together with citations from Derrida and Klossowski, Faulkner, and many others. At this point, the writer's discourse merges with Nietzsche's so closely that it turns itself into literature. But it is a very distinctive kind of literature that displays itself as a composite of multiple layers of citation, wordplay, allusion, and analysis. Here, at the latest, one could speak of the postmodernization of the reception of Nietzsche in philosophy.[17]

It is here, over the issue of "the postmodern turn" in philosophy, that the North American debate among Nietzsche specialists in response to Kaufmann bends back upon itself and

[17]See in this regard two articles by Alan D. Schrift, "Genealogy and/as Deconstruction: Nietzsche, Derrida, and Foucault on Philosophy as Critique," in *Postmodernism and Continental Philosophy*, ed. Hugh Silverman and Donn Welton (Albany: State University of New York Press, 1988), 193–213; and "The Becoming-post-modern of Philosophy," in *After the Future: Postmodern Times and Places*, ed. Gary Shapiro (Albany: State University of New York Press, 1990), 99–113.

is reinscribed on a second level of discourse. On this second level, "Nietzsche" is taken as a figure instrumental in the articulation of one's own philosophy and may or may not correspond to the image constructed by specialists. Two examples will suffice to describe this other debate.

Allan Bloom marks the first position in the debate over Nietzsche with his *Closing of the American Mind*. Undoubtedly Bloom's most polemical statements are directed against Nietzsche, whom he sees as one of the great prophets of contemporary life but an example of the dangerous potential everywhere visible today. Bloom does not reject Nietzsche out of hand, however; rather, he admires him in a contradictory way.

For Bloom, Nietzsche was an outstanding thinker, but Americans have been too quick to forget the political consequences of his thought. The hidden danger of Nietzsche is that Americans have naively accepted his "value relativism," while forgetting the horrors of Nazism involved. "We are like the millionaire in *The Ghost (Geist) Goes West* who brings a castle from brooding Scotland to sunny Florida and adds canals and gondolas for 'local color'" (*C*, 153). Nietzsche's pessimism in particular is too difficult for Americans: "A very dark view of the future has been superimposed on our incorrigible optimism. We are children playing with adult toys. They have proved too much for us to handle" (*C*, 195). What seems to disturb Bloom above all is the ironization of Nietzsche's thought that occurs, for example, in Derrida's *Spurs*.

Despite these cautionary evaluations of the political moment, Bloom sees Nietzsche's principal contribution in the same general terms as Kaufmann. For Bloom, "Nietzsche opened up the great terrain explored by modern artists, psychologists, and anthropologists, searching for refreshment for our exhausted culture in the depths of the darkest unconscious or darkest Africa" (*C*, 206). His work, though unfortunately political, was mainly humanistic, psychological, or cultural. Ultimately, it was rehabilitative as well: "Nietzsche restored something like the soul to our understanding of man by providing a supplement to the flat, dry screen of consciousness" (*C*, 207).

Certainly, Bloom's image of Nietzsche is incomplete. It lacks a thorough consideration of many of the texts, major themes, and the secondary literature. But this incompleteness arises because Bloom's argument is not principally about Nietzsche. It deals, rather, with the "educational crisis" in American schools today and uses Nietzsche as an instrument of diagnosis. Bloom's Nietzsche is not only part of the sickness but also part of the cure.[18] The image of Nietzsche he projects is highly ambivalent from the outset. He combines the features of Kaufmann's with those of other critics who have emphasized the politics.[19] Nevertheless, it is indicative of Nietzsche's growing importance that his writings would be used for such an analysis, as Richard Schacht has pointed out: "Bloom has probably done more to convince more people in this country that Nietzsche somehow *matters* in an important way than have all of us in the Nietzsche business, from Walter Kaufmann to the present company, put together" (*NANS*, 18).

Quite in contrast to the high seriousness of Bloom's Nietzsche, Richard Rorty's "has a sense of humor" (*NANS*, 13). To be sure, Rorty admits, there is a Nietzsche—"one of the worst of the various Nietzsches"—who seeks to legitimize the importance of philosophy for history (*NANS*, 13). But Rorty's Nietzsche is "less professionally deformed"; that is, he takes himself and his profession less seriously (*NANS*, 14). He has both a sense of his own uniqueness and "a rueful appreciation of blind contingency" (*NANS*, 14). He knows, for example, that the Americans might have had a successful revolution

[18]See Werner J. Dannhauser, "Remarks on Nietzsche and Allan Bloom's Nietzsche," *NANS*, 3.

[19]See, for example, Stern, *A Study of Nietzsche*; Sokel, "Political Uses and Abuses of Nietzsche in Walter Kaufmann's Image of Nietzsche" (both cited in note 20 to Chapter 3); and Terry Eagleton, *The Ideology of the Aesthetic* (Oxford: Basil Blackwell, 1990), 234–61.

even if Locke or Rousseau had never written a line or that with Plato, "very weird and unlikely things can happen," such as philosophers becoming kings (*NANS*, 14). Rorty's comments provide a model of his image of Nietzsche *in nuce* and demonstrate some of the ways in which he uses this image to support his larger argument. For Rorty, like Bloom, seems compelled to enlist Nietzsche in his cause. Whereas Nietzsche may have until recently been avoidable, he seems to have become a pivotal figure for understanding where we, in this case English speakers, have come from and where we may be headed.[20]

Rorty's most extended treatment of Nietzsche appears in *Contingency, Irony, and Solidarity* (*CIS*). Although this book has not had the mass-market appeal of Bloom's, it has touched off considerable debate in the humanities. Its image of Nietzsche could perhaps be described as a composite of features derived from both Kaufmann and Derrida: on the one hand, Rorty's Nietzsche is important as a "self-creationist" or, in Kaufmann's vocabulary, as someone arguing for "self-overcoming," but on the other hand, this "selfhood" is purely a result of "blind contingency," a centerless, changeable assemblage of desires and beliefs. Both the concept of a centerless self and the irony Rorty uses to describe its qualities parallel Derrida's treatment.[21] Above all, Rorty's Nietzsche will, like "William James, Freud, Proust, and Wittgenstein," be used to illustrate what Rorty calls "freedom as the recognition of contingency" (*CIS*, 46). Rorty's Nietzsche will be taken seriously not for his politics, as was Allan Bloom's, but for his

[20]On a similar topic in terms of recent politics, see Robert Eden, "To What Extent Has the World of Concern to Contemporary Man Been Created by Nietzschean Politics?," in *Nietzsche heute* (cited in note 11 to Chapter 3), 211–25; see also Peter Heller, "Concerning the Nietzsche Cult and Literary Cults Generally" (cited in note 22 to Chapter 3).

[21]For Rorty, the mediating figure for these dual predecessors was Alexander Nehamas: "My account of Nietzsche owes a great deal to Alexander Nehamas's original and penetrating *Nietzsche: Life as Literature*" (*CIS*, 27).

nearly Freudian awareness that "progress results from the accidental coincidence of a private obsession with a public need" (*CIS*, 37).

Admittedly, Rorty's Nietzsche resembles Bloom's as a figure caught between two conflicting demands. For Bloom, Nietzsche's "value revolution" is both part of the sickness of contemporary culture, in that it seeks to overthrow Enlightenment rationality, and part of the cure, for it allows one to see how dangerous such a revolution can be. But Rorty gives the opposite evaluation to the two sides. Nietzsche for Rorty is marked by both a "boundless sense of humor"—namely, at the point when he is aware of the effects of contingency—and a snobbish sense of his own world-historical importance (*CIS*, 108). Whereas Rorty would want to keep that sense of humor, he would prefer that Nietzsche "*privatize*" his world-historical project (*CIS*, 197).

In short, recent North American readings of Nietzsche have sought to modify Kaufmann's picture in many different directions. Just as, in French and German, Heidegger's massive yet oscillating systematization of Nietzsche has been modified or refined, English-language readings have sought to alter Kaufmann's interpretation in varying ways. In the process, the contributions of Deleuze, Foucault, Derrida, Kofman, and Klossowski have been adapted or criticized according to the demands of the argument. Danto, Magnus, and Schacht, each with his own suggestions, offer principles different from Kaufmann's as alternative bases for understanding Nietzsche. Nehamas and Krell highlight to differing extents the roles of Nietzsche's many styles. Bloom, among those who use Nietzsche for other arguments, retains the humanistic-anthropological emphasis and adds a critique of the politics; Rorty downplays the politics and drops the belief in a foundational human nature. But for all of these writers, and Heidegger was one of the earliest to recognize this feature, Nietzsche is a major provocation. My point is that far from seeking a "final" or "definitive" image of Nietzsche, it may be more useful to provoke further debate. "Philosophy has made no progress? If somebody scratches where it itches, does that count as progress? If *not*, does that mean it wasn't an authentic scratch, or not an authentic itch? And couldn't this reaction to the irritation go on for a long time before a remedy for itching is found?"[22]

[22]Ludwig Wittgenstein, *Vermischte Bemerkungen* (Frankfurt: Suhrkamp, 1977), 165–66.

Index

◁▢▷

Index of Names

In this index an "f" after a number indicates a separate reference on the next page, and an "ff" indicates separate references on the next two pages. A continuous discussion over two or more pages is indicated by a span of page numbers, e.g., "57–59." *Passim* is used for a cluster of references in close but not consecutive sequence.